TACKLE
SOCCER
THIS WAY

TACKLE
SOCCER
THIS WAY

DENIS LAW

STANLEY PAUL
London

STANLEY PAUL & CO LTD
178–202 Great Portland Street, London W1

AN IMPRINT OF THE HUTCHINSON GROUP

London Melbourne Sydney
Auckland Johannesburg Cape Town
and agencies throughout the world

First published 1965
2nd edition August 1968
This edition 1971

This book has been set in Times type, printed in Great Britain
on antique wove paper by Anchor Press, and
bound by Wm. Brendon, both of Tiptree, Essex

ISBN 0 09 105740 X (cased)
     0 09 105741 8 (paper)

CONTENTS

ILLUSTRATIONS

facing page

ONE

APPROACH TO THE GAME

I don't think I'm a 'big head'. It may look that way just because I haven't got a very big body.

I'll admit, though, to a feeling of vain satisfaction on learning of my selection for the Rest of the World team to meet England at Wembley on the occasion of the English F.A.'s 100th birthday celebrations.

Of course, during my professional career I have been privileged to take part in several highly significant matches for my club and country. Such honours as we have won on those occasions I have regarded as wholly due to team effort. As for the games themselves, I enjoy my football no matter whether it takes place at Wembley or on the practice pitch.

But this was something different. My selection alongside such legendary giants as Puskas, Di Stefano, Santos and Yashin meant full recognition as an individual. So perhaps I might have been excused for telling myself: 'This is it, Denis. You've arrived!'

Somebody worked it out that the sixteen players who represented the Rest of the World at Wembley on Wednesday, 23rd October 1963 had won 663 caps between them. That didn't surprise me, for Puskas alone could boast eighty-four for Hungary and five for Spain.

Two million pounds was the total sum for which we were insured.

We met together at a Kensington hotel, trained at White City and played one brief practice match against Chelsea at Stamford Bridge. With a smattering of English and Italian I tried to make friends with star players from eight different nations, while they wrestled with my native Aberdonian tongue.

'Interpreters are not necessary,' our coach Fernando Riera told the Press. 'The ball is our interpreter.'

This was true on the field of play. Doubts had been expressed about our ability to fit together as a team, but stars like Di Stefano, Eusebio, Masopust and Djalma Santos combine instinctively in close harmony —better than many who have played alongside each other for years.

A hundred thousand fans at Wembley that sunny afternoon will testify to what a good game it was. I agreed with Jimmy Greaves when he said: 'This was no exhibition, but one of the hardest and most satisfying matches I have played in.'

The first half, I thought, was pretty even. After the interval we seemed to lose some of the rhythm we had built up; understandably since five substitutions were made in our team. Any substitute needs time to accustom himself to the tempo of the game, and England were not in a mood to give anything away.

Mind you, I agreed with Harry Cavan, the Rest's chief selector, who said: 'This match can only be played once, and we think that the public want to see the best of the world's players.' Bringing on five substitutes at half-time allowed such great stars as Soskic, Eyzaguirre, Seeler, Puskas and my fellow-countryman Jim Baxter to share the honour of appearing on this memorable occasion.

A fine goal by Greaves, after a run by Bobby Charlton

in the closing minutes, gave England a well-deserved victory. Five minutes earlier I had converted a brilliant move by Puskas to make it 1—1, but it was clear that a draw wasn't going to satisfy our opponents as a suitable birthday present.

I have never seen England play with such determination, accuracy and skill, and most of the cheers were for them as Jim Armfield and Co. formed a guard of honour through which we left the field.

What I like to think is that this match proved that the best football is not necessarily English, Continental or even Scottish. It is intelligent and accurate ball artistry, and skill of movement off the ball, by players of all nationalities who are masters of their profession.

The object of this game of ours is simply to score more goals than the other team. The methods used are often devious in the extreme. But on this particular occasion I think that both teams showed that there is no reason at all why victory should not be pursued in an attractive and entertaining manner. . . .

The journey I made to Wembley on the great occasion I have just described was full of exciting incidents. It started for me on the back streets of Aberdeen where I was born on February 24, 1940.

As an undersized little shrimp wearing round-lensed spectacles I first learnt to control and kick a ball. Throughout my schooldays I lived for match days, when a certain amount of natural ability with a football and a lot of pent-up energy seemed to transform me from a midget into a giant.

On leaving school at the age of fifteen I set out across the border to try to carve a future for myself in English football. Huddersfield Town was my first professional club, and there I spent happy years building up both physically and mentally. By the age of eighteen I had won a regular place in Town's league side, and before my nineteenth birthday my first cap for Scotland.

Then the urge to get still further ahead set my feet wandering. I moved to Manchester City to experience First Division football and then to Torino to try my luck with the highly paid Continental stars of the Italian League. In 1962–3 I returned home to join Manchester United and share in my new club's Cup Final success towards the end of that season, and their many tense battles in English and European competition which have followed.

Many of my most memorable moments were those in which I wore the dark blue jersey of Scotland in home internationals, and World Cup encounters—particularly at Hampden.

But it seemed to me that the F.A. birthday match brought eight action-packed years in professional football to a rewarding climax. So let me stop there for a moment.

After all, this isn't just a book about me. It is about you and your own ambition to play amongst the stars at Wembley. That is what I should like to help you do, but you must appreciate right from the start that I can only help you to a limited extent. All the theory in the world can't make you a better footballer than you have been born to be. All I can do is to encourage you to practise as frequently as possible in order to make the most of what you have got.

Perhaps I can point out from my own experience. I shall also try to interest you in some arts of team-play.

A sound knowledge of all the skills employed in the game, and the ability to perform them accurately and instantaneously, is essential.

But this alone will not make you a great player, no more than technical skill makes a great photographer, or familiarity with words and their meanings a great writer.

Professional photographers tell me that they use a camera as if it were a third hand. The twiddling and adjusting of knobs and switches are automatic. It is their individual approach to the object in view that determines what sort of pictures you get.

It is the same in football. You have got to be able to read the game quickly and intelligently to know what skill to apply and perform it with flair and judgement at the right moment to achieve success.

When the ball comes within your range in the heat of a game there is little time available to consider how it can best be brought under control, or whether your shooting position is correct according to the textbook. These things must be automatic.

Unlike such players as Bobby Charlton, George Eastham and David Herd, I do not come from a foot-balling family. Therefore I cannot wholly subscribe to the view that football talent is inherited. Neither my father nor my four brothers have any particular ability for the game.

On the other hand, Bobby and brother Jackie picked up quite a few tips from the famous Milburns, who are uncles, and George and David from their equally famous dads.

I'm an exception in another way too. Most players I know live, talk and practically breathe football. They talk about games and players, past, present and future, endlessly from morning to night. Well, while I claim to get as much enjoyment out of an actual game as any of them, and do my full whack of training, once it is over the last thing I want to talk about is football.

I learn something from every game I play, and I'm still learning. But if I earned my living as a plumber I wouldn't want to bore my family with endless chatter about waste pipes and wet and dry joints all evening, would I?

Others will tell you that if you want to succeed you must dedicate yourself entirely to football, thinking of nothing else. This to me is sheer slavery. The more intelligent lads who are now making football their profession do not need to impose such rigid self-discipline. Indeed, I say that their love of the game will not lessen, and they are likely to be able to express themselves more fully on the field if they exercise their minds and bodies in other directions from time to time.

One thing I do think, though, is that once you make up your mind to make the grade as a professional you should put everything you have got into it. Keep up your outside interests by all means, but never to the extent that they interfere with your football.

As a youngster I made the mistake of dabbling in various outside jobs with a view to improving my security. I soon found that I would have done better to put all my energy into learning the one trade I had chosen for myself. Had I failed I would still have the youth and strength to turn my hand to something else, but the chance of failure would have been greatly reduced.

Later on, once you have made the grade, you can branch out into business, or a part-time trade, and you'll find—as I have done—the reputation you have built up in football is a big help outside.

But, as I was saying, I don't think that you can state categorically that footballers are born not made. There is a bit of both about it. You need a certain amount of natural ability to start with, and then the right sort of coaching in order to bring it out.

I emphasise the phrase 'right sort of coaching' because the wrong advice early in one's career could prove disastrous. Bad habits once acquired are extremely difficult to shake off.

From my observation the standard of coaching in Europe and South America is extremely high. Those coaches know how to get the best out of their players. Britain, too, has some good coaches, but I think our general standard is less advanced.

Like me, I suppose, you started kicking a ball because you enjoyed doing it. Nobody told you to do it, or how to do it. So right from the start the thing that drove you on was your love of the game. This is going to be your strongest asset.

The next thing, perhaps, is fitness. I don't think normal boys have much to worry about there. The exercise and running about you do every day of your life adds up to a formidable training programme.

And as for diet, no dietician has yet succeeded in devising a menu better suited to you than Mum's cooking.

When I was a boy I played football every day. You could say, more or less, I coached myself, for no one showed me how to play. I don't feel I suffered any particular disadvantage. At this stage of your development no one can show you how to control and kick a ball. You find you can do it or you can't.

Some boys might profit from being given a few short cuts, and I'll get round to this later in the book.

A little later you need coaching in team-play, and let's hope that you are as lucky as I have been in having such gifted and experienced advisers as Bill Shankly and Sir Matt Busby to show me where I have been going wrong.

There is a lot of boloney written and discussed about soccer. It is a very simple game when not cluttered up with theory and conjecture, and the common-sense approach is nearly always best. Do the simple, obvious things, but learn to do them better, quicker and more accurately than the other chaps can cope with.

What I would like you to aim at is to become not just a useful winger, half-back or full-back, but a complete footballer perfect in every department. This may not prove possible, but in aiming for the ideal and falling short you can still end up better than most.

1 *Kicking the dead ball* With the non-kicking foot parallel to the ball, head down, eyes firmly on the ball, Denis ensures an accurate, low shot.

2 *Kicking the dead ball* Changing feet, Denis shows the position of the ball in relation to the non-kicking foot with the knee of the kicking foot over the ball.

3 *Heading the ball* Again, the golden rule—eyes on the ball—the neck muscles taut, chest and shoulders braced.

4 *Heading the ball* Denis Law gets above the defence to head for goal.

TWO
YOUR KIT

———————

'The smarter you look, the smarter you play.'

How often have you heard that remark? It's true I never feel like playing my best if there is a tear in my jersey or my stockings keep falling down to my ankles.

Even in training, neatness leads to greater efficiency. I wouldn't want to train in a shabby tracksuit, whereas in the best gear I feel that only my work can justify it.

See how immaculate any professional team looks when it takes the field. Much thought and experiment has gone into equipping the players as perfectly and comfortably as possible.

The standard of their kit may be above the means of junior teams. But you can at least ensure that what you wear is clean, comfortable and in good repair.

But even before we start to discuss equipment there is something even more basic to demand your attention —your feet. These being the tools of your trade, as it were, they must always be given special attention.

Like most players, at the start of each new season I soak my feet in a solution of permanganate of potash, which one obtains at a chemist's shop. This helps to harden them.

Should I develop a blister I immediately take off my boot and get a bandage for the affected part, which I keep on until the trouble has cleared up. Blisters may

B

seem nothing, but they can be one of the worst handicaps to a professional footballer.

I bathe my feet regularly, being careful to dry between the toes afterwards to avoid athlete's foot (which can become very dangerous) and to apply talcum powder. I always keep my nails neatly trimmed.

Finally, change your socks as frequently as possible. All these things may seem obvious, but you'd be surprised how few players give their feet the full care that is necessary.

With the modern type of boot, a long and careful breaking-in process is unnecessary. But I never wear a new pair of boots straight away in a match. I usually wear them first for training, and put them on without stockings but with plenty of soft soap on my feet to avoid blisters. After that I wear them for a couple of practice games and they are ready for anything.

When I was first picked for my school side my parents couldn't afford to buy me football boots so I had to borrow a pair from the boy next door. It isn't a method I would recommend except in a dire emergency.

Many parents tend to buy boots for youngsters on the principle that the stronger and sturdier they look, the more economical they will prove. This could be false economy. Boys' feet grow so fast, anyway.

The modern boot is lightweight, of Continental pattern, and though it may cost a few bob more it is a good investment. I think it best for players of all ages because it allows more movement and comfort. Comfort is the important thing. If you feel comfortably shod you play better and enjoy the game more.

Personally, I choose new boots half a size smaller than the size of my walking shoes to get a tight fit. After a couple of weeks the leather expands and the boot moulds itself to the exact pattern of your foot. But with growing boys it is perhaps advisable to go for a really comfortable fit, as their feet stretch as much as the boot does.

If you can afford it, it is best to equip yourself with a pair of rubber boots as well, for when grounds are hard; or at least get a pair of leather boots with interchangeable studs. You can screw in the type of studs which suit the conditions on any particular day.

When the going is heavy I wear a long stud to get a better grip on the ground, while short studs are better in the wet. In that Cup semi-final we played against West Ham at Hillsborough in 1964 the pitch was so muddy it was like trying to run in black treacle, and if we had been wearing long studs we might all still be stuck there!

I don't like bars. They tend to make you slip. I always put on my right boot first, but this is simply superstition. Most players have a pet fad of this kind, and a set ritual to put their nerves at ease when preparing for the kick-off.

I lace my boots right up to the top, put the lace underneath the boot for two turns and then tie a knot round the back of the boot. If you tie the lace at the front of the boot you'll find that a kick on the knot can be painful.

Every good player I know is very particular about his boots. They are an individual responsibility. For international matches shorts, stockings and numbered shirts are provided, but players are expected to bring their own soap, towel, shinguards and boots, which must be properly studded.

After every match or practice, boots must be cleaned and allowed to dry naturally. Modern boots should not be coated with dubbin, but treated with polish like a walking shoe. Keep the studs in constant repair, making sure that nails do not protrude. Probably the most serviceable, hard-wearing stockings are those with a mixture of wool and yarn which stand up best to machine laundering. Hand laundering will give them a longer life, of course.

I keep up my stockings by tying a piece of bandage under the turnover, making sure that the knot is on the outside of the leg. If you tie the knot on the inside you tend to stop free circulation and cause cramp.

Shinguards won't stop you breaking a leg, but they do give protection against painful raps on the tender portions of the leg, so I advise you to use them. Incidentally, I believe that they were invented by a Notts Forest forward named Sam Widdowson, and first mentioned in the laws of the game in 1880.

After fastening the boots, shinguards should be pushed down inside the stockings as far as they will go, to rest just inside the front of your boot tops.

Personally, I prefer not to wear superfluous bandages, only using them when my knee or ankle has been injured and is likely to be unstable. Players who get into the habit of wearing elastic bandages find after a while that they rely on them.

We have come a very long way from the days when players wore caps, cricket shirts, long trousers and very often long flowing beards! These days the tendency is for lighter and lighter apparel. British international kit weighs slightly under four pounds and that of some Continental countries even less. But we must strike a compromise since many of our home games are played on very chilly days.

Football shorts are made in three sizes with specially

cut leg length and a strong, half-inch elastic in the waist-band. Shorts with wide hips are best to allow free movement.

Make sure that the elastic round your shorts is not too tight. You mustn't be handicapped in any way if you are going to give your best.

Goalkeepers, by the way, are obliged to play in distinctive colours of scarlet, royal blue or green, or white. In international matches they wear deep yellow, and this is also the colour for Scottish cup-ties.

A word about eyesight. As a boy I suffered from a squint and was forced to wear and play football in ordinary spectacles. They didn't bother me too much, but would have been a hopeless handicap in professional football.

Fortunately for me, at the age of fifteen I was able to have an operation to cure cross-eyed vision and have never had to wear spectacles since.

If you have to wear glasses I would advise you to tape the frames to the sides of your head, or wear one of those bands round the back of the head which fasten to each end of the sidepieces.

In football of a higher class spectacles would prove an impossible handicap, and the answer for you must be contact lenses. At the start of his professional career Willie Henderson, the great right-winger of Rangers and Scotland, played in contacts without any bother. Indeed, he spotted goal chances quicker than most of us. Willie's eyesight improved, however, and he no longer needs artificial aid.

There is one other article of the game worthy of your attention—the ball. This is something of no little importance, you'll agree, yet how few bother to study it?

Historians tell us that Roman soldiers played a game

not unlike soccer during their occupation of the country; the ball they used was of cloth or leather stuffed with flock, called harpastum.

The name 'football' was first used to describe an inflated pig's bladder, covered with leather made by shoemakers, which was big enough to be kicked about in public-school games. A Frenchman described it as a ball made of leather which was 'as big as the head, and filled with wind'.

Later, about 1870 we are told, rubber took the place of the pig's bladder for inflating the ball.

The best footballs made today are made from hide, impregnated with oils to give them life. The hide is cut into panels which are stitched entirely by hand. The larger number of panels in a football—and therefore the smaller the area of each—the less risk there is of distortion. Most balls today have eighteen panels.

F.A. rules say that the ball must weigh no more than sixteen ounces nor less than fourteen ounces at the start of a game. Its circumference must be not less than twenty-seven inches and not more than twenty-eight inches.

A football is an expensive item, so if you are fortunate enough to own one of your own, look after it. After play wash all the dirt from the ball by holding it under a running tap. After bouncing it to get rid of surplus water, smear dubbin over the surface while the ball is still inflated.

If the ball is white or orange it has been specially treated with a coating of plastic, so don't apply dubbin under any circumstances. Soap and water is the answer in this case.

Deflate the ball and let it it dry naturally, never in front of a fire. And don't over-inflate—a ball should never be 'board' hard.

I've been reading recently that one manufacturer has made available a special football boot which is so designed, he claims, as to make ball control a much easier matter.

I'm sorry—but the only way I know of improving ball control is through practice. Boots, important though they are, have nothing to do with it. Indeed, judging by the skill of some of the South Americans we have seen, there is a strong argument in the theory that ball skill is best learned in bare feet, the theory being that the feet mould themselves to the shape of the ball.

However, ball skills are the subject of my next chapter. See that your equipment is right, and you are ready to play.

THREE

THE BASIC SKILLS

Learning to kick the ball accurately is the first step towards playing good football—that may sound as obvious to you as saying that you need to breathe to stay alive, but it does need stressing. So many boys start off kicking the wrong way, and, indeed, not all senior players are as accurate as they should be.

Basically, the action is to kick against your own weight, while balanced on the standing foot.

The instep is the part of the foot which normally comes in contact with the ball. To keep the trajectory of the ball low, the normal requirement in a game of football, the knee of the kicking foot must be well over the ball at the moment of impact. The non-kicking foot should be close to, and alongside, the ball, toe pointing the way you want the ball to go, knee bent. Your body-weight should be evenly balanced and distributed, arms half spread and eyes glued to the ball.

The kicking leg is swung from the hip, knee fully bent, toes pressed down and back. The kicking leg swings forward naturally and follows through with the toe continuing to point at the target. The curve of the foot where the boot is laced is the point which should meet the curve of the ball on impact.

Remember—keep your head down and practise your timing.

When you have to lift or chip the ball (for a corner or

a pass over the head of a defender) you alter your balance slightly, placing the non-kicking foot behind the line of the ball.

This causes the impact to take place later in the swing, the kicking knee is not over the ball and contact is made on the bottom half of the ball, giving an up-and-under effect. Your body is balanced slightly backwards.

Kicking a moving ball needs keen timing and judgement so that you get as near to the position you would have for kicking a dead ball. To volley, keep your eye on the ball and your body over the ball and just hit it, which you can't help doing if you get into the proper position.

Getting power into your kicking is not just a matter of brute force, but more to do with good timing, which can be achieved only by practice. You must have seen big burly players who don't get half as much power in their kicking as smaller lads who combine timing and physical force. I have.

For a starting test you should be able to kick a dead ball with the instep of either foot at least thirty yards, allowing one bounce. Naturally, everyone has one stronger leg that he tends to use naturally. In my case it is the right.

Obviously a two-footed player has the advantage. We all know of stars who use one leg exclusively for standing on (Puskas was one), but your aim should be to develop every part of your game.

Some people develop the weak foot by wearing only a gym-slipper on their stronger foot during practice games. In my case I always tried to *think* two-footed, never saying, even to myself, that I could kick only with my right.

Kicking a ball against a wall with your weak foot will

25

bring it on—even if it's only a tennis ball. I always used to carry one about in my pocket and even when my brothers were inside the manager's office at Huddersfield Town, fixing up my professional future, I was out on a cobbled street, kicking my tennis ball against the back wall of the grandstand.

In a game the first thing is to get the ball down to your feet as rapidly and tidily as possible. Experiments will show you that the best way is to deaden the ball with whichever part of you is handiest—head, chest, knee or thigh—and, having stopped the ball, to withdraw that part quickly so that the ball drops straight down.

Sometimes you will need to kick first-time, but to achieve absolute accuracy it is always best to get in command of the ball before starting a movement.

Basically, the inside of the foot is used for trapping. Early contact is made with the side of the foot, which is then quickly withdrawn. Anyone who has played cricket will know that you take the pain out of catching a fast ball by pulling your palms back as you take it, letting the ball hit a yielding surface. That is how your foot should deaden the ball. You can practise this by having a friend throw a ball at you from different heights and speeds until you can kill it every time—and, eventually, can kill and move forward with the ball at the same time.

You should also try trapping the ball with one foot, making a return pass with the other, and alternating feet each time.

For a ball that comes too high for feet or legs you must use your chest, bending your trunk back from the hips and getting your chest under the ball, if it is high, or forcing it down with your chest if it is low. Always remember to let your chest 'give' on impact.

26

Moving balls below knee height are best trapped with the inside of the foot, although the sole, instep or outside of the foot can be used as variations.

Get the foot at right angles to the way you intend to go with the ball. To move left, you use the inside of the right foot and *vice versa*. The other foot is placed in line with the oncoming ball so that on impact it will be just behind the ball. Your trunk leans forward to the left and your weight is balanced on the left foot.

The right leg is then thrust forward, knee bent, toes upwards and outwards. On contact the curve of your foot is wrapped round the curve of the ball to persuade it in the intended direction.

These are all movements which will come naturally to anyone who has learned to master the ball. Often you see players go off on their own to juggle with the ball, and you may think that they are showing off. It is true that some of the tricks you see are not much use in a game, but I can assure you that this sort of practice will help you considerably by enabling you to do straightforward things with more confidence. The ball must be your servant, and here I think all British players can learn a lesson from the Continentals.

To achieve this, try such exercises as rolling the ball on to the instep and keeping it balanced there. Then let it bob gently up and down on your foot.

Try passing it from left to right foot without it touching the ground, a trick which helps towards co-ordinated footwork.

Then throw the ball from the foot to the head, balance it there and let it drop to the foot again, next time catching it on the thigh and balancing it there.

So much for ball control. The ball wizard who can keep it up for 300 times on the trot is no good to his team if he cannot pass the ball. Pass—not just thump long balls up the field, a common failing in schoolboy teams.

I think it was in the very first international ever played between players representing Scotland and England that the outside world realised that Scotland had invented what seemed like a fantastic football move. Instead of rushing through in a pack, every man for himself, they made ground by kicking the ball from man to man. All sorts of ancient people may have had games that included kicking round objects (even human heads, it is said) but it was we Scots who gave the world the passing game that is modern football. So much for patriotism.

Even at the age of nineteen, when I was a Scottish international, I was still guilty of trying to run the ball all over the field, beating man after man on my own. My manager at Huddersfield, Mr Bill Shankly, made me realise I would achieve more by intelligent passing—and also conserve my energy for the full ninety minutes.

For passing you use the instep, the inside and outside of the foot, the sole and the heel. For all passes, except very long ones, I prefer the inside of the foot, which gives widest possible foot area in contact with the ball, thus giving greater accuracy.

To make this pass you again try to get the standing foot alongside the ball, but turn the kicking foot sideways, making contact with a pushing action. A full follow-through helps both timing and direction and that is why I do not favour the stabbing pass.

Eyes on the ball again, of course—in time you will be able to obey this golden rule and still manage to see where you are passing without losing concentration.

You will frequently come up against the situation

where there is no one in position for a pass (I will deal with running into position later on) and you have to dribble the ball forward, beating at least one opponent before you can pass.

You can practise dribbling at speed by setting up skittles, or other markers, ten feet apart in a straight line and going round them at speed, using both feet to keep the ball firmly in control.

Next, get a partner to back away from you while you advance with the ball, trying to keep a consistent distance of two yards. Run with the ball, then stop suddenly, at the same time drawing the ball back with the sole of the boot. Immediately you push it forward with your heel and run on.

The art of beating a man is to persuade him that you are moving one way, and when he has committed himself by moving his weight to the wrong leg you move the other way as fast as possible.

The head is also used for passing and every footballer should set out to develop his heading powers. You use the forehead, keeping both eyes open and on the ball until the moment of impact, at which the neck muscles must be tightened.

To head downwards, tuck the chin in and meet the top half of the ball with a forward, downward movement of the forehead, getting the ball squarely in the centre of the forehead or it may fly off in any direction.

For a high header, used mainly by defenders, you strike the bottom half of the ball with a forward-and-upward motion, trying to get contact on your hairline, where even the heaviest sodden ball will cause little pain.

Hurdling helps the right muscles for heading and is good for timing as well. Your stomach and neck muscles are important: one good exercise is to lie on a mat with a medicine ball gripped between your ankles. Swing your legs up and over till they touch the ground behind your head.

Another is to grasp the ball in outstretched hands, with your trunk inclined backwards. Pull the ball hard on to your forehead, at the same time letting your trunk and head come forward quickly. You head it out of your own hands, noting the increased distance you get with practice.

Any number of players can practise heading the ball to each other without letting it touch the ground. You are making progress when you manage six consecutive headers.

Another form of practice is hanging a ball from a beam, raising the height the ball is from the ground until you can get at least thirteen inches above your own height. Heading tennis may be easier for you to arrange. You will find that it is important to space your feet for proper balance and to wait for the ball with head inclined backwards. You shoot your head forward to punch the ball forwards with the forehead, taking care not to wince or let the ball hit you—it doesn't work and it hurts.

The last basic skill I will deal with here is good tackling. The secret is timing. When you go in your object is to block the other man's pass, then bring your leg through quickly and strongly to take the ball away. Get your body-weight well over the ball so that you can use your tackling foot with force and bring your shoulder into play.

Crouch slightly so that your own balance is not upset by impact, and play the ball with the inside of the foot. Try to get face-on to your opponent—forwards try to shield the ball from you with their bodies and a tackle from behind is always liable to be a foul.

Some professional players specialise in heavy bodily contact in tackles—others seem to have mastered the art of timing so well they just lift the ball from the other man's toes. In all things my advice to you is constantly to practise *every* move of the game, even the things you are best at. It is always possible to achieve *better* balance, *better* rhythm. In a game go looking for jobs to do—try to attract the ball to you. Run to meet it and learn to control it quickly and efficiently.

Use your feint or your dribble to beat a man and make a pass. Keep moving into positions where you can receive a pass. If you lose the ball fight to win it back.

These are golden rules which apply to all players, no matter their ages or their positions.

FOUR

HOW TO MAKE THE BIG-TIME

There's a story told about a fifteen-year-old boy from Glasgow who showed such great promise at football that Mr Stan Cullis, then manager of Wolves, took him on the groundstaff and for three years gave him all the coaching he could. When the boy was eighteen it was obvious he would not make the grade as a professional and he was sent back home with a sympathetic letter from Mr Cullis.

The boy's father replied to the letter: 'I'm sorry you couldn't make him into a footballer,' he wrote, 'but thank you for making him into a gentleman.'

This happened some years ago, before the abolition of a maximum player's wage and before the present attitude of regarding professional football as a fine career for even the best-educated boys. I think it tells you something about what could happen to a youngster in football even in the so-called 'cloth cap' days.

The tendency to make football a real career, just like any other job or profession, has increased recently: in 1960 the apprentice professional scheme was brought into existence in England; clubs are now allowed to sign schoolboys before they are fifteen, giving them expert coaching and advice while they are still at school so that, if they want to, they can become apprentices when they reach fifteen.

Just imagine that you have been playing with your

5 *Heading the ball* Timing your leap is the basis of successful heading. Denis takes off to meet a cross at Highbury.

6 *Collecting the ball* Chest inclined forward, head over the ball, Denis raises his right leg immediately before killing the ball with the inside of the right foot.

7 *Collecting the ball* Willie Henderson of Rangers shows the position of the foot and leg at the moment the ball is killed. Both knees are slightly bent and arms are extended to aid balance.

8 *Collecting the ball* Pulling the upper part of the body backwards, Denis lets the ball strike his chest so that it will not rebound.

school or youth-club team and a scout from a big team approaches you. He comes to see your parents. He says that you have a future in the game.

You have probably dreamed of becoming a big-time footballer, but now you are faced with reality: the door is slightly ajar. What should you do?

Perhaps I can give you some help in making up your mind. I was spotted playing for Bowis Secondary Modern School in Aberdeen. I was fifteen. I had a squint and wore spectacles. I weighed eight stone nine pounds. I was five foot three inches. Mr Andy Beattie, who was then manager of Huddersfield, took one look at me, standing between my two big brothers:

'Havers, the boy is a freak,' he said. I suppose he wondered how his brother, Huddersfield's Aberdeen scout, could ever have imagined this scruffy, squinting youngster was a footballer. Nevertheless, he took me on as a groundstaff apprentice at £5 a week. I was put in digs with eight other apprentices. It happened just like that. I made my league début at sixteen.

Should you follow in my footsteps?

I can think of no other way of life that could have done so much for me as football, but every individual is completely different and all I can do is point out the advantages (and the disadvantages) of becoming a professional soccer player. Today the earning power of the soccer player has vastly increased since the days of the £20 maximum. Weekly wages of £100 are not uncommon in the English leagues and the top Scottish clubs. A Jaguar is now a common sight in the players' parking space.

Of course, the further down the leagues you go, the smaller the income is—but if you are the type who starts off thinking that he will never reach the top, then I advise you to think of another career. Football is not an easy life in many ways, and you need boundless faith in yourself.

Apart from the money, football is one of the best ways I know of turning boys into men: travel broadens the mind, they say, and any footballer who gets even near the top will find himself travelling with his country or his club in countries he would possibly never have visited otherwise.

As an apprentice professional you will get all the help you need to learn the game and I think we can take that for granted. You will also have a certain amount of educational activity, so your parents need have no worry about you having nothing to do but stand about street corners all afternoon, or haunt billiards saloons and low dives.

What does the future have in store for the boys who do make the grade? Lets take thirty-two as a fairly average age for a player to have gone as far as he will ever go in soccer, the time when his body begins to slow down and he begins to think of giving up the game.

Many players go on longer, but it would not be wise to take Stanley Matthews or Gordon Smith as anything more than unique cases. Now that ought to have given you at least fifteen years as a professional.

In that time you should have used the advantages of your position to make some kind of future for yourself outside the game. You should have been able to save enough money to launch yourself into a new career, always supposing you are not one of the minority who stay in football as managers, trainers or coaches.

I have invested in one or two business enterprises. I did this because it seemed the sensible thing to do, not because I am obsessed with my future. Football is a young man's game and if you are the type who worries at the age of fifteen about pensions you should try the Civil Service instead. However, you can be sensible.

My advice is not to combine football with another job until you have established yourself as a player. Look at it this way: football demands, certainly in the beginning, everything you have, physically and mentally. I don't think your teenage years are the best for trying to cope with two jobs, two sets of worries. If you don't make the grade by the age of twenty, when you ought to have a pretty good idea of your abilities, then you are still young enough to turn to something else. If you do make the grade there's no need to get panic-stricken about the fact that football is all you know. On a smaller scale it's like asking one of the Beatles what he is doing to safeguard his future!

Injuries? You take that chance, of course. But you do in any job. More accidents happen in the home than in any other sphere of life. Does your mother worry all the time about accidents?

My advice is—have a go. Imagine a man of thirty, in a safe job, who turned down a chance of football fame because he preferred absolute security. I am sure he would regret it for the rest of his life.

There are all sorts of obstacles to be surmounted even if you become the biggest star in the game. Establish any kind of reputation and you are a marked man on and off the field. Your life tends to become public property. Every game you play will be rigorously watched by the gentlemen of the Press, and they will sometimes write things about you that will make you want to crawl into a corner—if you are silly enough to take them to heart.

And there is always the moment which comes to us

all—when you know you are finished. Footballers 'retire' at an age when many men are just beginning to get somewhere in their careers. You are young and old at the same time. You just accept this as an inevitable fact. We all grow old.

I have enjoyed every minute of my career as a professional footballer. To me it is the greatest adventure in the world.

I wish you as much luck as I have had.

FIVE

GOALKEEPING

Like lots of forwards I know I like to try my hand in goal during practice matches, not only because the change is a bit of fun (and anything which makes training easier to bear is welcomed by me!) but because it also gives me some idea of scoring goals from the other viewpoint.

Bobby Charlton is another Manchester United forward who often plays in goal in practice and from the way he dives about I would say that he could well have been a very good goalkeeper if that had been his original position.

However, there is a great deal of difference between practice matches and the real thing, and of all the positions in a football team I think I would like the least, goalkeeper is it. The responsibility is fantastic. Any other player can get through a bad game without actually losing the match for his team, but an off-form goalkeeper, standing as he does in the last line of defence, can not only create uncertainty throughout his team but his mistakes are usually goals. One of the best (or worst) examples of this was a certain match at Wembley a year or two ago between England and Scotland. I had one of the poorest games of my international career, and I don't think there is any member of the Scottish team that day who can look back with anything but sadness. The England inside trio of

Greaves, Bobby Smith and Johnny Haynes were at the peak of their form and I doubt if many teams would have held England on their form of that black afternoon (for Scotland). They won 9—3. Yet although none of us played to standard, the spotlight fell on our luckless goalkeeper, big Frank Haffey of Glasgow Celtic. It was very hard lines on Frank—who has proved before and afterwards that he can be a great goalkeeper (his display in the 1963 Rangers–Celtic Cup Final at Hampden was, I am told, almost miraculous). But this is part of the cross the goalkeeper has to bear. It can happen the other way round.

Few Scotsmen who are old enough to remember that far back will forget the name of Jimmy Cowan of Greenock Morton, who put on one of the greatest displays of goalkeeping ever seen in this country at Wembley in 1949. Time and time again Stan Mortensen and Raich Carter, the famous England inside men, fired point-blank shots—only to be thwarted by Cowan. Scotland won that game 3—1. Jimmy Cowan, I believe, was one of the first post-war goalkeepers to make a science out of his goalkeeping: at the start of a match he would drag his heel along the ground from the penalty spot to the centre of the goal-line, giving himself a clear marker on which to base the angles at which he covered his goal.

The greatest keeper I ever saw was Bert Trautmann, the German who held the fort for so long at Manchester City. Not only was Bert a wonderful acrobatic goalkeeper, he was one of the most intelligent goalkeepers I have ever played in front of. He never wasted a clearance and in my days at Maine Road his accurate throwing and kicking gave me many goal chances.

Most of the time my job is to outwit goalkeepers and

as a forward I find that the most difficult to beat are the thinking keepers, the ones who read my mind and position themselves intelligently to forestall my intentions. This is the kind of goalie who seldom has to throw himself about the goal making spectacular saves —he is generally so well positioned that the ball seems to come straight to his arms. Yashin of Russia, who played in the England–F.I.F.A. match at Wembley, is like that, and so is Gordon Banks of Stoke City. The spectacular goalkeeper who seems to spend the whole match flying through the air is not the best— either he is making hard work for himself by failing to anticipate intelligently, or else the opposing forwards are firing in long easy shots which give him a chance to show off.

Goalkeeping came into being in 1870 when the rules were changed to allow one player to use his hands, and to this day that one player is the real specialist of football. Not many boys want to be goalkeeper, probably because he is stuck between the posts for ninety minutes with, perhaps, only five minutes' actual participation in the game.

Jack Kelsey, the great Welsh goalkeeper who played so brilliantly for Arsenal until injury prematurely ended his career, once told me that his theory about boys and goalkeeping was simply that in all groups of boys there is one to whom it is more natural to catch the ball than to kick it. Jack could never remember a time, even in street games, when he wasn't going for the ball with his hands.

I would compare the goalkeeper's job—and the nervous strain that goes with it—to that of a champion golfer who is putting for victory on the last green—only the strain goes on for ninety minutes. Goalkeeping is a

39

job for a specialist, someone with wonderful reflexes, for the ball moves very fast near goal and the keeper has to be able to go this way or that—and change his mind—with only a fraction of a second in which to make his decision. You don't always have time to position yourself in advance.

The first requirement is a safe pair of hands which can take a ball cleanly. You can practise by throwing a ball against a wall and catching the rebound. Safety first should be your motto, and there is no point in an agile leap at a ball if you cannot hold it firmly when you get it. Because of the safety-first rule you should generally tip a ball over the crossbar or round the post for a corner rather than risk a mis-save, which could deflect it into the net, or a shaky landing which leaves you vulnerable to a shoulder charge into the net.

As goalkeeper you should make sure that your team knows to give you an early touch of the ball in every game—especially on a cold or wet day. The keeper's first touch of the ball is vital and it is far better that he gets it from a friendly passback than from a shot fired in anger.

The next most important role the goalkeeper has to play is domination of the penalty area. A keeper who can do this gives his team great confidence. The first test of whether you do dominate the area is the cross. The position to take up is at the post farthest away from the wing from which the ball is coming. This gives a wide view of the goalmouth and penalty area. As soon as you see the path of the ball you must go for it single-mindedly, ignoring the distraction caused by other forwards and getting up with confidence to take the ball with as high a leap as you can manage. If you are having to jump among a bunch of players the best plan is to punch or push the ball out to the wing, but otherwise your aim should be to catch it cleanly, bring it down to your chest (for protection against the shoulder-charge) and then be ready to use your feet to avoid onrushing forwards.

A goalie should never allow himself to be caught with the ball in his possession. There is a growing tendency *not* to shoulder-charge goalkeepers, but this is still allowed by the rules and there will always be some centre-forward who likes to try the old-fashioned shoulder-charge. Others will merely keep running in front of the keeper as he tries to get into a clear space for his downfield kick. Remember, four paces are allowed between each bounce of the ball—try to improve your footwork until you can evade the forwards and get the ball away within those four paces.

A goalkeeper needs another quality—courage. He needs to have the kind of guts that will enable him to dive fearlessly at the feet of a forward without thinking of his own safety (although experience helps you to learn the safe way of diving forward—with one shoulder and arm slightly forward to protect your face). Some players say that good goalies need to be a little bit mad, and I think they are referring to this special brand of courage that the keeper needs. One of the finest examples of this was shown by Bert Trautmann in the 1955–6 Cup Final at Wembley when the blond Manchester City keeper went on making fearless saves with a broken neck!

What do you do when a forward has burst through your defence and is running in on goal with only you between him and the net? You must move out immediately towards him. With each yard you narrow the shooting angle and make it more difficult for him to decide which way to shoot. This is where Jimmy Cowan's line came in useful—he could always tell where he was in relation to the centre of the goal. It needs great accuracy to chip a ball over the goalkeeper at speed, considering that the ball has to rise about eight feet and then come down in the net. Very difficult—as a forward, I can tell you that.

If the forward decides to shoot you have given him very little space on either side to aim at and your own speed will give you extra momentum for a dive to either side.

If he tries to dribble the ball round you, stop moving forward but stretch your hands forward to smother the ball, diving in his path if need be, but always remembering to dive only when you are absolutely sure which way he is going. A goalkeeper on the ground is practically helpless. In the chapter on captaincy I describe how the keeper is placed on his knees on the goal-line and a team-mate throws the ball at him from close range, giving him practice in getting off the ground quickly.

The keeper's job has really only just started once he has saved the ball. He then has to initiate attacks by his own side and here he should know exactly where his team-mates are so that he can use the ball accurately and quickly. A quick throw over the heads of the opposition to the wing can send your forwards away in a flash with half the opposing team stranded in your penalty area. I prefer the throw to the long kick because it is generally more accurate: a kick can easily go too far. Use the over-arm javelin throw for the long ball and the under-arm roll for the short.

Among good goalkeepers I have seen and whom it would be worth your while to study are Gordon Banks of Stoke City, Peter Bonetti of Chelsea and Alex Stepney of Manchester United.

On the whole I like a big goalkeeper and Bert Trautmann, at six feet and thirteen stone, seemed to me to have the ideal goalkeeping physique. Two things in particular helped him become a great keeper: in his native Germany he was a very skilful handball player (basketball is also good practice for a keeper), and during the war, as a paratrooper, he learned how to fall in every possible way without hurting himself.

He also had intense powers of concentration, which is important: no goalkeeper can afford to pick daisies when the ball is at the other end of the pitch. He must continually 'read' the game, watching for the quick breakaway that might leave him the only man between the forward and goal. He must even be ready to run halfway down the pitch and kick the ball clear if a long ball looks like leaving an opponent with a clear run to goal.

Most league goalkeepers do some of the training with the rest of the team and then spend time on their own doing gymnastic exercises to strengthen stomach and arm muscles.

Already I have explained that the golden rule is to keep your eye on the ball. This applies especially to goalkeepers. One second's break in concentration and the ball may be in the net.

The goalkeeper must develop a close understanding with his defenders and in any training session the centre-half, two full-backs and keeper will practise on their own, acquiring an understanding of what to do in the various situations that commonly occur in a game. There should be a clear understanding, for instance, that a certain shout from the goalkeeper means that the ball should be allowed to come through to him. Full-backs should never turn their backs on the keeper when he gathers the ball, for goals are fairly frequently scored by alert forwards nipping in to intercept a thrown clearance that a defender is not anticipating.

In the gymnasium the keeper should do vaulting and agility exercises, abdominal exercises on a sloping bench, tug-of-war and wrestling to strengthen the grip, and plenty of work with the medicine ball to strengthen the hands and arm and shoulder muscles. Undoubtedly, regular handling of the ball is the most important training of all.

You will see in most league games today that modern goalkeepers prefer the short goal-kick just out of the box to a defender, who then taps the ball back, to the long goal-kick downfield. This gives the keeper a chance to show greater accuracy in his goal-kick clearances— but you should not forget to practise goal-kicking as well. There will be occasions when the opposing forwards make it impossible to take the short-passing goal-kick.

The modern tendency is to bring the goalkeeper more into the game, with half-backs making use of fairly long passes back to start an attacking move. However, the goalkeeper is still very much of a specialist and if you like responsibility and have the necessary courage (or 'madness') you will find it one of the most rewarding positions in football.

SIX

FULL-BACK

In the old days in Scotland there were several full-backs with impressive nicknames like 'The Bull' and 'Killer'. I can remember 'Tiger' Jock Shaw, of Glasgow Rangers, who played the way you might think from the nickname.

Football is a rapidly changing game and I cannot think today of one first-class full-back who goes in for the red-blooded, do-or-die, clear-your-lines-at-any-price style of game which gave birth to these nicknames.

Remembering my spectacles and my lack of height and weight, it is difficult to imagine that I started my career with Kittybrewster School, Aberdeen, as left-back, but I did, and I enjoyed tussles with goal-hungry forwards—the bigger the better. However, my inclination was always to take the ball upfield and have a go myself and this tendency made our sports master, Mr Wright, switch me to the forward line.

You just *didn't* go upfield as a full-back in those days. Most of the time you were supposed to tackle hard and heavy and get the ball upfield with as big a boot as possible.

Today Mr Wright might not have moved me, for the whole conception of full-back play has changed. So many full-backs have developed the art of dashing down the wing that we forwards are beginning to wonder if everybody wants to get in the act.

I can think of Terry Cooper of England and Leeds,

Ray Wilson formerly of England and Everton, Tommy Gemmell of Celtic and Scotland, and several others who are often to be seen nipping down the wing for a cross or a shot at goal. Tommy Docherty, when he was manager of Chelsea, worked out a whole attacking plan based on Eddie McCreadie's speed and ball control which enabled him to wait for a forward pass and then take the ball down the left-wing in a way that would have been regarded as blasphemy twenty years ago.

In football it's the exception that proves the rule—but I believe that first you must steep yourself in knowledge and experience of the basic rules before you can branch out, and I would tell any young player to learn the basics of full-back play before he starts the fancy stuff.

Today's full-backs must be fast because they have to face wingers who seem to be getting faster every season. I can imagine wingers like Jimmy Johnstone of Celtic or Peter Thompson of Liverpool making hay against those bull-like characters of yesteryear, and they have disappeared to make way for a new, skilful player who can play his part in attack.

The first thing a full-back must do is, however, defend. He is directly opposed to a winger and this is his first responsibility. When that winger is on the ball the full-back has to stop him—not by pulverising body-rushes or sliding tackles (a very specialised art best left to those few players who seem to slide as accurately as they walk).

The knack is to know when to tackle. Go in too quickly at the wrong moment and the winger is past you, heading clear for goal. Wait too long and he'll have brought the ball far enough up to be within striking distance of your goal.

The basic insurance for the full-back is at all times to

make sure the winger is forced out to the touchline. Don't face him head on, but take a position slightly to his inside, giving him only one direction to take—outside you, along the touchline.

Out on the wing he can do less immediate damage and has less room to work the ball.

Of course, defence is not an individual responsibility and you will find your team conceding fewer goals if you work with the other full-back and your centre-half on what is called the swivel system.

The centre-half is the pivot of the swivel. The full-backs are its arms. If the opposing right-wing is moving towards your centre-half, then your right-back should move in to cover the centre-half. *Vice versa* if the attack is coming from the left. As a forward I know that the shortest route to goal is down the middle, and unless there is a full-back moving in behind the centre-half I am in with a great chance as soon as I am past the pivot.

The two full-backs should never play square (be on the same line), because in that situation your defence has nothing to fall back on when a fast ball is sent between the two backs. The general rule is that when one moves forward, the other moves back: when one moves outside, the other moves in. When your goal-keeper goes out to a high ball, one or both backs should fall back on the line to cover him.

I think that positional sense is the real key to success as a full-back, and this is something that you can really only learn by playing the game. The secret is to know the exact moment to commit yourself to a tackle—and then to be ready to turn and race back if you are beaten, trying to get between your man and the goal again.

Few players run as fast with the ball as they do without it and unless you have gone into an unsuccessful sliding tackle you stand a fair chance of catching up the winger.

These days it is not just enough to be a defensive full-back. I do not think it will be long before crowds actually jeer any big kick: already first-class backs go through whole games without really having a hefty boot at the ball. The fashion for short-passing, intelligent back play began in recent years when Sir Alf Ramsey, England team manager, played for Spurs, and was carried on by such full-backs as Eric Caldow of Glasgow Rangers, Jimmy Armfield of Blackpool and Nilton Santos of Brazil.

Ray Wilson when at his peak with Everton was, I would say, actually the best individual back in Britain. He was so far removed from the old idea of the big clearance that he actually could not kick a ball particularly far, but his reflexes were so fast, his interception and use of the ball so intelligent, he was a major force in any team he played for.

Coming out of defence with the ball, the back can either push it out to his deep-lying winger and run inside for a return pass, or push the ball ahead of his wing-half. The modern style is to play your way out of defence —not kick the ball upfield. Possession of the ball is all-important these days and, while there are still some soccer spectators who bawl at you to 'get it up the field', I think everyone is coming to realise that it is more sensible to be in possession of the ball in your own half of the field than to boot it into your opponent's penalty area.

None of this should be taken by you as a sign that the tackle is out of date. It never will be, and the full-back must be able to tackle purposefully and cleanly. It is

9 *Passing the ball* Tommy Baldwin, the Chelsea forward, shows how it's done.

10 *Passing the ball* Body leaning in the direction he wishes the ball to go, Johnny Haynes uses the inside of his right foot to make a pass to his left.

11 *Passing the ball* Even as he prepares to take the ball forward, Haynes makes a quick survey of the field, looking for unmarked teammates or for open spaces into which they can run to receive his pass.

12 Denis Law shields the ball from Tottenham Hotspur back Cyril Knowles.

not a position for someone who fears bodily contact. The secret is to choose your moment—particularly when the winger is on the foot nearest the touchline so that he has nothing to fall back on. Go in for the ball with your foot turned outwards, your body-weight well over your legs, creating the maximum blockage to a quick flick forwards by the man you are tackling.

It's the ball you are after, remember. I have seen many teams lose goals because their defenders went for the man instead of the ball. Go in hard—you stand a greater chance of injury if you go in half-heartedly.

Use the shoulder by all means if you are running side by side with a winger, but your main consideration is the ball. Kick into touch for safety only where there is nothing else you can do, for most modern teams have clever moves at throw-ins which make them almost as dangerous as corners near your goal.

Full-backs seldom get the publicity and the glory that fall to players in other positions, but they play a vital role in any team, and I am sure that as soccer becomes more scientific their importance will increase. In 1963 the two full-backs of the Italian club Internazionale of Milan scored twelve goals. In Italy that's quite a total. It looks as though the backs *are* getting in the act.

SEVEN

WING-HALF

Just before I took the field for my first international match at Hampden Park, Glasgow—for me the greatest ground in the world—Sir Matt Busby, then the Scottish team manager, told me that I had a special responsibility for marking Danny Blanchflower, the Irish right-half.

'You must keep a close watch on Danny,' he said, 'because he is the principal source of danger. He will collect loose balls from defenders and throw-outs from the keeper and try to start moves—as he does with Spurs. Stick closer to him than his shirt.'

'Right, Boss,' I answered.

I followed my instructions so enthusiastically that Danny's legs were black and blue after the game (which Scotland and Ireland drew 2—2—the year, 1958).

I mention this match because it may give you some idea of the relationship between the inside-forward and the opposing wing-half. Naturally, being a member of the defence, the wing-half usually marks the other team's inside-forward, but the roles are interchangeable when you have a wing-half like Blanchflower who plays a key part in attack.

In the eleven men who make up a football team everyone is important but some are more important than others and the most important of all are the wing-halves. It is impossible to think of any great team which didn't have great wing-halves.

Scotland is particularly blessed with class players in this position, with Billy Bremner (Leeds), John Greig (Rangers), and Bobby Murdoch (Celtic) all fighting for a place.

The wing-half is crucial to a team because he is the link between defence and attack, the man who brings cohesion to the game. Perhaps I am wrong in talking about 'the' wing-half, for the right- and left-half of any team are a pair and they are most successful if they work as a pair.

My own preference is for a pair of wing-halves who know their own roles—one primarily a defender, the other one an attacker. The Scottish combination of the attacking Baxter and the defending Greig or Crerand was ideal, in my opinion. No team can really afford two attacking wing-halves; if they are both up the field they will leave a great vacuum in which the other team's forwards can work in freedom. Neither can a team afford two purely defensive half-backs, because that robs the team of the middlemen who do the fetching and carrying for the forwards.

I have played against the grimly defensive half-back who stands close enough to me all through a game to be almost standing on my heels.

I do not like this at all, selfishly, perhaps, because this kind of player spoils my game completely, but also because he spoils the game as a spectacle for the people on the terracing.

However, you are not at the stage where pleasing a crowd is of any importance. Your greatest need is to master the game for its own sake—and if you are a half-back you must learn what your role should be.

Now there may be occasional games where the other team has an inside-forward so fantastically brilliant that he deserves the full-time attentions of a wing-half—but I doubt it very much. By reducing himself to a completely negative role he has robbed his own team of fifty per cent of its attacking ammunition. The wing-half is a danger man as long as he does not restrict himself to the job the full-back should be doing.

The prime qualification for a wing-half (after stamina, which his role as part defender, part attacker makes fairly obvious) is the ability to release the ball quickly and accurately. Occupying the middle of the field, his job is to break-up the other team's forward moves before they get within striking distance and then to start attacks of his own.

My friend Pat Crerand is one of the best passers of the ball in the game. He has mastered the art of kicking in a dead straight line for twenty yards or more, an asset which not only gives Manchester United tremendous advantage in mounting attacks but also relieves Pat of the strain of having to run long distances with the ball.

For a start you could practise hitting a dead ball in a straight line until you can hit a tree or a chalk mark on a wall nine times out of ten. Pat stabs the ball so that it travels hard and low, like a machine-gun bullet, to the forward. Danny Blanchflower had a different style of kicking—he flighted long, curving balls which penetrated deep into his opponent's defence, almost miraculously, it often seemed, finding an open space into which his own forwards could run on to the ball.

There is nothing miraculous about it. It's a case of hard work, experience and practice. Whether you follow Crerand or Blanchflower or Jim Baxter (who specialises more in short, incisive passes) the important thing is to be able to seize the ball in your own half and bring or send it forward to your own attackers. You are a general, deciding on the direction the attack should take.

One part of the wing-half game is taking throw-ins. We all know players who have fantastic throwing ability —like Dave Mackay of Derby, and Ian Hutchinson of Chelsea.

Not everybody is born with the knack of heaving a ball into the goalmouth from the touchline—but you can practise throws with a heavy medicine ball to achieve greater length. The most important thing is to find an unmarked colleague. In most cases he then returns the ball first-time to the wing-half, thus evading the opposition and giving the half-back time to plan an attacking move.

The main thing to watch about the throw-in is to make sure that your hands take the ball behind your neck before releasing it—otherwise it is a foul throw. With your feet astride, knees bent, swing the arms forward— without taking your feet off the ground. If you are trying for distance you will lean your trunk back as you prepare to throw.

My own philosophy about throw-ins is to get the ball back in play as soon as possible, although you will be able to do this only if your team-mates get into position to receive the ball. This movement is the most important part of the throw-in and to my mind one of the most pathetic sights in any game of football is to see a wing-half standing on the touchline, bewildered by the fact that there is no one near enough to throw to.

Stealing distance at throw-ins is a fairly common habit. I think it is a complete waste of time and, if the referee spots it, can only lead to another hold-up while you are sent back to the proper position. I am irritated by anything that holds the game up and I am sure it annoys everyone else, too.

When your own goalkeeper is taking a goal-kick you as wing-half should take up position about ten yards inside your own half: for goal-kicks by the other team's goalie, about five yards from the inside-forward you are marking, which will be somewhere about the centre circle.

At corners the wing-half should take up a close-marking position beside the inside-man he is against. If the corner is at the other end he should be about ten yards outside the other team's penalty area, ready to seize half-clearances and send the ball back into the goalmouth or to an unmarked forward.

Much of the half-back's success depends on whether he has a natural instinct for when to intercept passes, when to tackle—and when it is right for him to come up the field in attack. When I say instinct, I do not really mean you have to be born with the knowledge. It is something you acquire from playing the game.

More than anyone else a half-back has to think on the move. Goal-scoring forwards may look faster—but they are generally acting on reflexes, which are automatic. If they score once in every ten attempts they are doing well. The wing-half needs to be a lot more accurate than that.

He has to use his imagination, knowing whether to switch play by a long ball out to the opposite wing (and that is just one of the occasions which needs really accurate kicking) or to stab a short one down his own wing, run inside for the return and then push the ball through to his centre-forward.

Just one word of advice—it is not always the best thing for a young player to mould his style on the best professional playing at the time. Stars like Billy Bremner are unique—and they do many things which would be disastrous for a young player to try.

If you can gather a ball quickly, trap perfectly, keep running for ninety minutes, tackle *and* dribble, hit a bouncing ball thirty yards to a colleague—and also be ready to get up in attack to seize the odd chance—then you can take it that you have the basic qualifications for playing wing-half.

You are still not necessarily a *good* wing-half, for on top of these qualifications you must have imagination. You are the general of the team, the backroom planner. You are the brains *and* the muscle.

Football is always going to be just that little bit more hard work for you as a wing-half than for anyone else in the team.

EIGHT
CENTRE-HALF

When Ian Ure, the giant centre-half with the blond hair, left Dundee in Scotland to join Arsenal most of the London club's supporters expected him to work some miracle with the Gunners' rather leaky defence.

To their surprise Scotland's centre-half—the most expensive in this position—did not manage a miracle. Ian himself knew that he had a shaky time in his first games in England. Like many first-class Scots who move south, he found the pace of the English game much faster.

But there was another obstacle which Ian had to clear before he settled down to command Arsenal's defence.

At Dundee Ian played centre-half in the old scheme of things, the pivot who stands with his full-backs behind him on either side and who dominates the centre of his team's defensive area.

Some people thought they could see a reason for a slight unsteadiness in Ian's play at Highbury in the fact that he was asked by his new club to adapt himself to the double centre-half system. No longer was he the sole master of the middle, given full responsibility for blocking the road to goal.

I want to tell you more about the double centre-half and 4–2–4 in another chapter, so I will just say that Ian Ure found himself having to work shoulder-to-shoulder with a player who was, in fact, a second centre-half.

This must have been unsettling for a man used to being his own master—and it gives you some idea of the new complexities that have entered the life of the centre-half.

There is no doubt that the centre-half is the kingpin of any defence (or should be). Many boys are given the job because they are big, hefty lads—in the popular mind *all* centre-halfs are rugged giants—but if you remember Billy Wright of Wolves and England you can see that it's not absolutely necessary to be over six feet tall. It helps, though. The centre-half has a great deal of heading to do. On average he will have to head the ball out of his own goalmouth about ten times in a match, so that is one department of the game in which you *must* be proficient if you want to play pivot.

Opinions differ on whether centre-half is a difficult or an easy position. Several famous wing-halves have put years on to their playing careers by switching into the middle, where there is a great deal less running to do.

Some centre-halves seem to be able to stroll through a game, but this is a sure sign of a pivot who has developed the sense of anticipation to a very high degree. The centre-half, in his pivotal position, has the best actual view of the game and he must use this advantage to the fullest.

I think it is essential that you develop a mental attitude of *command*—you are in charge of the middle of the field and you must always feel that you are dominating your particular area.

If you are not a particularly fast runner you must compensate by learning how to intercept or tackle at a moment which gives the opposing forwards no chance to receive the ball and turn towards your goal. Once the centre-forward has trapped and turned *you* are under a handicap, because you will have to make a turn and a quick sprint if he passes you.

Many centre-halves like to make their tackles or interceptions just at the moment when the centre-forward is receiving the ball. At that particular moment the centre-half is able to use his view and, unlike the player he is challenging, he does not have to worry about changing direction once he does get the ball.

At all times you must be 'reading' the game, taking up positions that will leave you able to deal with whatever forward move the other team's forwards will make. A few yards out and you will yourself be hopelessly out of position, perhaps with a ball bouncing over your head, having to make a turn—while the centre-forward can have a straight dash past you.

This brings us to your partnership with the two full-backs.

The three of you should always be covering each other. Suppose your left-back has gone out to the wing to block the approach of the right-winger: it is your job to cover anything the winger does with the ball on the inside of the back. You must be prepared to fall back quickly to meet a high cross—or to move up and intercept a ball pushed inside your full-back to the inside-forward.

If this means you move slightly out to the wing your other full-back must then move in correspondingly to cover you.

The centre-half role has changed in recent years. No longer does the pivot content himself with getting the ball, taking a couple of steps and then banging it down the centre of the field. Centre-halves like Ian Ure, Billy McNeill (Glasgow Celtic) and Mike England (Spurs) rarely use the long kick for the sake of clearing their lines.

Having stopped an attack, the centre-half's job is to give the ball to his wing-halves or inside-forwards. *They* do the fetching and carrying: your job is stay in your position. Of course, you may, by reason of your commanding viewpoint of the game, see a chance of sending a long ball to one of your wingers so that defence can be turned into attack as quickly as possible.

I would advise any centre-half to concentrate on immediate distribution of the ball and to leave dribbling to other people. You, remember, are guarding the quickest route to goal and a dribbling mistake can give the other team a dangerous run-in on your goal.

What do you do if the centre-forward, the man you are immediately opposing, starts wandering out to the wing?

The answer is — don't follow. Many centre-forwards deliberately try to entice the centre-half out of the middle of the field and if you fall for that you will leave a dangerous gap in what is the most vulnerable area of the field. The wing-half should go out to cover the centre-forward, leaving you to use your height and strength in the box.

The greatest centre-half I have seen was John Charles, now player/manager of Hereford. To my mind a complete footballer, he was used by his clubs and his country at centre-forward, but I think centre-half was his best position. His all-round mastery of the football arts enabled him to use his physical advantages without ever having to stoop to any kind of brute force or underhand tactics—and that, I think, is an ideal all footballers should have.

NINE

INSIDE-FORWARD

I was asked once to pick a team of the best footballers I have seen and for my inside-forwards I chose Jimmy McIlroy, and Ferenc Puskas, the great Galloping Major from Hungary. Now I'm not advocating that every young player should set out to be a carbon of his soccer idols—but a study of these two inside-forwards will help explain the role of the inside-forward—and will also illustrate the point that however much I generalise about the game, individual players can become top-class stars despite glaring weaknesses in their play.

The great Puskas had eighty-four Hungarian caps before he went to Real Madrid: there he won several Spanish caps, helped Real win the European Cup five times—and to avoid a defeat at home for six years. Yet by theoretical standards he was only half a player. He used his right leg to stand on and little else. Right up till he retired, he could still reveal flashes of the razor-sharp work in the goal area and the cannon-ball shooting which made him one of the world's finest inside-forwards.

Jimmy McIlroy is almost completely at the opposite end of the range of different inside-forward styles. A crafty general, he seldom scored goals himself—and admits frankly that nobody regarded his heading of a ball as a bigger joke than himself.

My advice to all young players is to work hard to improve any deficiencies in your game and you would be better off copying what these great players *can* do rather than consoling yourself that you, too, might be a great one-footed genius.

Inside-forwards can be classed in two styles—schemers (like McIlroy) or thrusters (like Puskas), depending on their own temperaments or the requirements of their team.

I did not choose inside-left as my position—my schoolteacher in Aberdeen told me that was my position and apart from a few outings at inside-right and centre-forward I have played there ever since. It suits my temperament because it is the busiest position on the field and generally I like to regard the whole field as my parish, playing my part in defence and attack, rather than be tied to one specific area of operations.

A good thing for a boy is to find out his own best role as he gets experience, starting off by mastering the general aspects of his position and letting the specialisation come later.

An inside-forward, perhaps more than any other member of the team, must be able to control the ball. He must have speed *and* stamina, for he not only has to mark the opposing wing-half but has also to mount attacks—and often finish them off.

He often finds himself closely marked with nobody near to pass to, and then he must have the ability to run and swerve and dribble his way out of trouble.

His passing must be highly accurate, because today's style of play requires more quick interpassing and running into position for the return than marathon individual dribbles. When I was a young player with Huddersfield I tried to dribble my way through whole defences—and this, I would say, is the commonest fault in any boy's play.

The fact has been brought home to me over the years —and this is a simple truth that cannot be repeated too often—that football is a passing game.

Let's take a common situation in a game. Your opponents are attacking, their forwards and wing-halves converging round your goal area.

As inside-forward you have already tried to block the advance of the opposing wing-half. Now you must fall back, not crowding into your own box, because an overcrowded defence can be just as inefficient as an undermanned defence. Your immediate job is to block any diagonal back passes to the wing-half. Remember, more and more teams are finding the way to goal in these days of massed defence by quick back passes to deep-lying wing-halves, who may then be in a clear position for shots at goal. Dave Mackay of Derby has scored many goals from just this kind of move, the Derby inside-men suddenly switching play from right to left, across the face of the defence, giving Dave a chance to go through on the clear side.

Once you intercept this kind of pass, or get a short ball from one of your full-backs, your job is to convert defence into attack. In modern football few players rush headlong into every possible opportunity for tackling and as soon as an inside-man has the ball many wing-halves will immediately drop back, giving him a few seconds to make his next move.

One of the most effective is the short passback to the full-back—who should be running away from his goal towards the wing. As soon as you have passed you take up position for a return. The full-back can push a short one to your winger—who has also fallen back, lying on the touchline. He can then give you a square pass inside, so that you have completed a triangle of passes around any opposing forwards.

Now you should be clear for a short run into midfield before your opposing wing-half closes in. This is the moment when you should have 'read' the game—summed up the positions of your own forwards—and should know whether a long crossfield ball to your left-winger or a sharp angled forward pass to your right-winger will bring better results.

Whichever you choose, it is then your job to move quickly upfield, ready for short inter-passing with your right-winger, or a return cross ball from the left.

Basically, an inside-forward should feed more balls to his own winger (inside-right to outside-right, inside-left to outside-left): I have sometimes been accused of starving my outside-left and this may be because I have a slight tendency to the right foot, which means I tend to get the ball and move inside. Johnny Haynes formerly of Fulham was another inside-left who tended to move to the right when he received the ball. Study films of him if you get a chance, because he was one of the best inside-men at hitting accurate reverse passes (i.e. in the opposite direction to the one he is going). By moving one way he got a defence turning to follow him—and the sudden change of direction gave his left-wing a chance to cut in behind the defence.

You can see that an inside-man must have the stamina for covering lots of ground, falling back and then going forward as play changes. But he also needs the ability for the short dash into the scoring position —and no successful inside-man can afford to let a thirty-yard run exhaust him.

Some teams use a particular inside-man for scheming

13 *Beating your man* Maurice Setters braces his body to meet a legitimate shoulder charge from Denis who braces his weight on his left foot.

14 *Beating your man* Using his fantastic body-feinting ability, Peter Thompson of Liverpool tries to entice his opponent into a lunging tackle, keeping the ball close to his own feet for precision control.

15 *Beating your man* Bobby Charlton of Manchester United versus an Arsenal defender. Swerving to the left, Bobby draws the right back to one side but . . .

16 . . . quickly reversing direction, Bobby is now in a position to move away with the Arsenal defender trying to come back into a tackling position.

and the other one for striking. John White and Jimmy Greaves when he was with Spurs were a typical top-class pair in this respect. Before his tragic death in 1964 John was the fluid master of the open space, the man round whom Spurs' attack swivelled. He generally tended to lie deeper than Jimmy Greaves, whose reflexes near goal are so deadly that no manager would want to waste him in a deep-lying role.

White created openings by using the ball. He rarely overworked it. On the other hand, top-class inside-men like Colin Bell and Johnny Giles of Leeds have such a flair for ball control that they can mount attacks by dribbling past the first line of defence.

Roy Vernon was a different inside-man again. He was one of those players who seemed to create an electricity as soon as he was in possession. Roy pounced on mid-field balls, and had such accuracy in kicking and running that he often had a choice of a defence-splitting pass to either wing or a shot at goal.

My own style is to try to suit my game to circumstances. If I am up against a wing-half who follows me closely all through the game I try to move about so much that he is drawn out of position, making space for my forward colleagues. In other games I have taken up a position on the halfway line, a foot from the touch-line.

This is useful against a team which goes in for all-out attacks. A long ball from either wing-half gives me a chance to collect and start a run for goal while most of the other team's defence is well upfield.

However, this is a rather sophisticated tactic and I would advise younger teams to play a more orthodox style. Remember, a First Division team plays together a lot longer than any school or junior team and tactics can

E

be built up over several seasons to suit the particular skills of the individuals in the team.

You can practise various aspects of the game, like throw-in tactics. Liverpool used one recently in which the wing-half threw the ball high to the inside-man, who headed it back over his opponents to the full-back, who had time to make a long pass downfield. They vary this by throwing to the full-back, who heads it forward.

Another point to remember is that, like a centre-forward, the inside-man receives many passes facing his own goal. He has to master the art of turning quickly with the ball. You can practise this on your own, hitting a ball against a wall and swivelling quickly with it under control on the rebound.

Of all the positions on the field, the inside-forward *must* set out to master all the football arts. On his shoulders rests most of the responsibility for creating the opportunities for goals—and that is what the game is all about.

TEN

CENTRE-FORWARD

I was saddened to watch Alfredo Di Stefano of **Real** Madrid show clearly in the 1964 European Cup Final that he had come to the twilight of his career. While he was still as assured as ever in the centre of the field, he failed to produce the brilliant exchanges of short passes in the penalty area and the electric finishing power which made him, for my money at least, the greatest centre-forward I have ever seen.

A man of tremendous stamina, the balding Di Stefano has always been without comparison as a centre-forward, so what are the qualities needed of any boy who fancies himself as a budding Di Stefano?

I could say it's goals that count, but even here you cannot generalise, for there are several first-class centre-forwards these days who rarely score. They lie deep behind the other forwards, acting as a pivoting source of through passes.

Ian St John of Liverpool used to play this game exceptionally well having such energy he not only seemed to act at times like a fourth half-back but was often up there to get the goals as well.

While my general attitude to the game is that it doesn't matter who scores goals, my preference is for a centre-forward who *is* a centre-forward and not a deep-lying distributor of the ball.

The centre occupies what is the most dangerous **area**

of the field and to my mind there should always be a man in there ready to head or shoot goals And it is largely futile for this player to be wasting energy chasing all over the field. Wander about by all means, particularly if you can draw the centre-half out of position—but make your wandering achieve something.

It can either put you in a good position to be unmarked when a pass comes out of defence or it can coax the centre-half away from his beat, giving your other forwards goal chances.

A centre-forward can practise the timing of his runs at goal with his team-mates, getting them to shove balls through his own defence so that he gets this timing right. It may not have occurred to you before, but this is absolutely vital if you are to be effective. Start your run forward too early and you will be continually whistled up for offside. Leave it too late and a defender will always be there before you.

I do advise you to concentrate on your role as a scoring centre-forward at this stage in your career. It is one thing for a professional player to fit into a special pattern—his manager knows why he is lying back and why he is not scoring a lot of goals.

You, on the other hand, are hoping to go farther in the game and you must learn to play an orthodox style which you can later develop and polish.

Your crucial area is in the penalty box. Outside of that you must be able to feed your wingers with long, sweeping passes and nod long balls from your own defence down to your inside-men. But you are going to make or break yourself depending on how you perform with the goal in sight.

The first thing, obviously, is to be near enough goal to snap up chances. These days there are few centre-

(Above) 17 *Beating your man* The secret of beating two men in a row, as Denis shows against West Ham is to keep the ball within a controllable distance at all times.

18 *Speed off the mark* Chris Simpkin of Hull and Tony Green of Blackpool race for the ball.

19 *Taking your chances* Denis shows the correct way to hit a first-time volley shot at goal. He has raised his kicking leg high enough to make sure the ball does not soar over the bar.

20 *Taking your chances* There's no time to fiddle with the ball in the goal area, says Denis, seen here hooking a first-time volley at goal in preference to bringing it down for a more accurate shot.

forwards of the old school, bustling, dashing heroes who tore through defences and shot home thirty-yarders: modern defences are too well organised.

Most of your chances come from short balls or missed clearances. Di Stefano and Puskas were probably the greatest exponents of the rapid exchange of short passes which can carve a way through the tightest defence. In this one of you acts as a 'wall'—your inside-forward hits a short one to you, lying almost parallel with him. You hit it back, while he has run ahead. You have completed a sideways 'V' of passes—with a defender left behind inside the 'V'. You can practise this with only two of you attacking and two defending, until it comes naturally both to judge your short passes and also how to act as the 'wall', so that the ball almost rebounds without effort from your foot in the correct angle to make your 'V' and bypass the defender.

Shooting is by far the most important single asset a centre-forward must have. Football is goals, that's what the game is all about and nobody likes to see poor shooting. In fact, I would say that a crowd can forgive almost anything or anybody except the forward who consistently fluffs his chances near goal.

A boy who wants to be a centre-forward can practise on his own, which gives him some advantage over the other positions. A blank wall is ideal. Chalk a set of goalposts about a quarter of the normal size and start shooting at them from all angles—*first-time*. You don't really gain anything by trapping the ball and teeing up your shots. This sort of chance rarely comes in a real game, where half-chances are more frequent.

As the ball bounces back from the wall get ready to volley or half-volley it straight back, at all times keeping it low (your chalked goals should be less than four feet high). With the volley you learn how to control your foot in the air, so that it is not swinging wildly—which almost certainly will produce a ballooned shot. If the ball bounces back too high for a kick, head it at goal.

With the half-volley, where the ball is kicked just as on the bounce, you must get your body over the point of impact, your non-kicking foot in line with the ball. At all times practise with both feet. I think it is much better to start off concentrating on accuracy and only when you get most of your shots inside the goal-markings to try to get more power in your kicking. Often a centre finds he is not shooting at the whole goal but at the narrow space left by an advancing goalkeeper. Then, at speed, you have to hit a low, controlled ball at one of two fairly small spaces. One tip here—many goalkeepers will advance in such a way that they leave a slightly wider space to one side. The temptation is to shoot at the most open side of the goal—and that is what the goalkeeper is expecting. He *wants* you to fall for his trap. Once your shooting is accurate you can surprise him by going for the narrower angle.

Remember also that it takes a goalkeeper longer to dive than to jump in the air: good low shots a foot or so off the ground are more profitable than spectacular drives aimed just under the bar.

The secret of good heading at goal is to jump so high that you are actually heading the ball downwards. Great centre-forwards of the past, like Tommy Lawton, Dixie Dean and Jimmy McGrory, scored hundreds of goals with the head because they mastered the art of jumping, timing their leaps so that at the point of impact they were nodding the ball down at goal.

There are many different styles of centre-forwards these days. There are hefty bustlers whose job is to take the weight of attack off inside-men who are less physically strong and to use their strength to open up defences (Bobby Gould of Wolves); there are silky manipulators of the ball who operate from behind the forward line (Allan Clarke); there are all-round centre-forwards who lead their lines, distribute well and snap up unlikely chances near goal (Joe Royle, Everton).

My tip to you is, as in every other position, to start off playing an all-round orthodox game until you begin to develop a natural style. The centre-forward is more often on his own with the chance of winning a game than any other player. He gets the glory—but he has to work for it.

ELEVEN

WINGER

One of the many things that Tom Finney of Preston North End and England fame could do was to cross a ball from the right-wing with his left foot at a time when any normal player would be angling for an opportunity to cross the ball with the outside foot.

This move requires a fantastic degree of balance and body control that few of us, least of all when we are boys, possess. To my mind Tom Finney was the greatest winger I ever saw. He had all the qualities any player must strive to master if he wants to be a top-class winger—he was incredibly fast on the ball, his ball control was perfect, his tactical sense brilliant and his shooting first class.

I play alongside different wingers and I suppose anything I say reflects to some extent my own personal taste in wing colleagues. My favourite wingers are Cliff Jones, formerly of Spurs, Gento of Real Madrid, George Best of Manchester United and Jimmy Johnstone, so you can see that I am not hidebound by my own particular style of wing-play.

Basically, there is no point in playing on the wing unless you have a fair turn of speed and good ball control. Most of the time you are going to be engaged in man-to-man sprints against the full-back and you do not have the time or the space of your colleagues inside.

A winger must be on the move all the time. He must shift with the play and of all the players in the side he is the one who will have to carry the ball longest distances. If he is static the game tends to become static.

Let us go through a number of the moves the winger can make in attack. My favourite is the winger who runs to the byline and then chips the ball back so that it comes to myself or the other forwards as we are going towards goal. It is always easier to take a ball that is coming towards you than one from the rear and this move gives a forward a particularly good view of the goal.

Another simple—but devastating—move is for the winger to take the ball right up to the full-back and, just before the tackle, to turn it back to his inside-forward (or wing-half). The latter should then push it through on the full-back's inside, giving the winger a chance to sprint forward on to the ball in what may well be a clear scoring position.

Most full-backs try to jockey a winger out to the touchline, where he is less dangerous because there is less he can do with the ball. I think it is always more useful for the winger to cut inside the full-back. Not only have you then got him behind you, where tackling is much more difficult, but you can go straight to goal or draw another man out of defence before slipping the ball to an unmarked colleague.

Often the winger is moving diagonally across the face of the goal and the defence lets him move untackled because he does not seem to be as dangerous as a forward heading straight for goal. This sideways movement can give you a chance of coming to a gap in defence through which you can try a shot.

Probably the greatest dribbler of all time was Stanley Matthews. In his heyday he could be surrounded by three defenders and still come weaving out of the trap with the ball at his feet.

Matthews had a knack of throwing the full-back off balance by moving in one direction so convincingly that the full-back committed himself to a tackle on that side. As soon as he did, Stan was going the other way. Because of this speed and ability to change direction he was able to show the back the ball, and as soon as the tackle was made, whip it away mysteriously. We called him the Hammer of the Scots, for he seemed to put on a special display of Matthews magic against the many left-backs Scotland threw in against him over his long international career.

Like all really dangerous wingers Matthews required the constant attentions of two defenders—one marking him and one trying to intercept passes before they reached him. If you can command this kind of attention from the opposing defence you will be doing your team great service on or off the ball. In general I would say that the best way to become a dangerous winger is never allow yourself to be pigeon-holed into any one move or style of play.

Always keep them guessing. Nothing is more boring than the winger who runs down the touchline and finishes every time with a high cross into goal. These high crosses are seldom profitable, in any case—and, like any move, it can be countered if the defence knows what to expect.

The first thing in any game is to test the full-back. Is his left foot stronger than his right? Then you'll beat him more easily by going round his left side.

Is he slower than you are? Then you can hit the ball past him and beat him in a straight sprint. Is he a bull-like tackler? Then you can hold the ball until he starts his lunge and then move smartly to the side.

Another move to practise is the run down the side of the field with the full-back falling back in front of you, back-pedalling, not wanting to make a tackle until he sees which way you are going.

Here you can keep him guessing by several changes of direction, encouraging him to turn this way and that until he is so far off-balance that you can go past him on the other side.

Common faults I notice among wingers are to drift too far into the middle of the field, especially when up against a defence that sticks inside. The great advantage a winger has is room and he should always be making use of the wide open spaces near the touchline.

He should never be so far upfield as to break the link between himself and the men behind him. He should always be ready to take a cross from his opposite number, being in a good position to run in on the blind side of the defence for a shot or a header. Often it's better for a winger deliberately to cross the ball right over the goalmouth so that his colleague on the other touchline can take advantage of the fact that the defence is facing the other way.

You must practise corners and crosses so that you can make them drop on the right spot and also to the stage where you can make them in- or out-swingers.

Obviously a right-winger can make the ball swing into goal more easily by using his left foot (*vice versa* for the left-winger) but by practice you should be able to in-swing with the foot nearest the byline. This is done by hitting the ball with the outside of the instep, the toes pointing at the ground.

After Spur's Alan Gilzean scored the winning goal against England at Hampden in 1964 the England manager, Sir Alf Ramsey, said it was not the kind of goal that should be scored in that class of football.

He meant that the old-fashioned corner, dropping about six to twelve yards from the centre of the goal-line, should be a gift for any good goalkeeper. This is why teams like Spurs concentrate on short corners, winger to inside-man, inside-man draws the full-back and slips the ball back to winger, who then has run along by-line to goal.

Even so, you must practise your crossing ability so that you can drop them in the right place.

A winger must do some defending: he marks the wing-half or inside-forward at throw-ins and he must harry his opposing winger by chasing him. At corners on the opposite side he must be lying ready for the short clearance, and on his own wing must mark one of the two men involved in the short corner.

I have seen the freedom that playing on the wing tends to give enable Bobby Charlton score many wonderful goals from the Manchester United left-wing. It can be one of the most exciting positions in the whole team.

Another move you can try is a 'scissors' attack: you take the ball and cut diagonally across the field towards the other corner-flag. At the same time your inside-man is ready to run the other way and as you meet you leave the ball with him, keeping running to draw the defence. He can then make ground before they realise that the whole attack has changed direction.

That great character of Glasgow Celtic, Charlie Tully, was so good at foxing defences he could send full-backs running after non-existent balls by suddenly pointing dramatically in the direction they thought he

21 (Above) *Taking your chances* Everything Denis has got went into this shot for goal in a match at West Ham. The kicking foot has come forward in a perfect follow-through, which is essential to the accuracy of your shooting.

22 (Below) *Taking the penalty* Rather than blast the ball at full force, Danny Blanchflower uses clever body feint to send Benfica's goalkeeper the wrong way. It was one of the goals that helped Spurs to beat Benfica 2–1 in their home leg of the European Cup semi-final in 1962.

23 *Taking the penalty* It's Jim Baxter. placing his penalty kick so shrewdly
that the Airdrie goalkeeper has no chance of saving it.

24 *Corners* Willie Henderson uses his right foot to
send over an out-swinging
corner. Again, you should
note how his foot and body
follow through to ensure a
smooth, accurate kick.

was going to pass the ball. Wingers should go in for the unexpected. It's no accident that some of the game's greatest personalities have been wizards of the touch-line.

TWELVE

TACTICS

A lot of new jargon has been creeping into football lately and I wouldn't blame any young player for being confused by constant references to 4—2—4 systems, linkmen, strikers, funnel defences—I am sometimes confused myself.

In the old days it was simple—the team had a pyramid shape going out from goal to the wings: forwards moved in a 'W' formation and you stuck to your own position. Today the shape of the team has changed —at least in many top teams, if not at junior level. If you play in a school team I imagine your sports master gives you such tactics as you use and I hardly imagine him relishing the idea of being told to change styles by one of his lads.

The importance of planning is to make best use of the players in a team. Many of these innovations are designed for specific star players and as few youth teams play together season after season it is hardly worth your while changing your natural game to adapt to some fancy planning operation.

But there are basic rules which in my opinion all teams could follow. The first rule is to stop goals being scored against you. The second is to score goals yourself.

The danger area to your team is the penalty area and if your team is under pressure you must funnel back to guard this area at all costs.

At Manchester United we do not believe in man-to-man marking. The nearest man takes his nearest opponent—producing an open game which is best to watch and best to play.

You mark a position—not a specific player (unless he is so particularly dangerous, like Danny Blanchflower when he played for Spurs, that he requires personal marking throughout the game). This means that forwards who switch positions cannot throw your defence into confusion.

The player nearest the man with the ball tackles—and if each member of the team has the correct idea about his own positional play you should have a compact defence.

In defence all eleven players are defenders (which does not mean that you all stand in your own penalty area) and in attack all eleven can play a part, including the goalkeeper with his throw-outs. Defenders must be able to play calmly out of defence with a series of quick, short passes (unless in real emergency). Forwards cannot stick too rigidly to the positions shown by the numbers on their backs. Numbers mean little today and five average forwards who have a close understanding and can therefore switch about to meet the needs of the moment can be far more effective than five stars worrying only about their own jobs. All five forwards should be capable of scoring, and should also be willing and able to turn instantly into defenders once their opponents have the ball.

It is far more important for young players to learn to play as a team in general terms than to bother about advanced tactical ideas.

However, it is as well to know what 4—2—4 means. The basic idea is to have a unit of four defenders, a unit of four attackers and two linkmen. Although many people have the idea that it is purely a defensive set-up, in reality it is designed to turn defence into attack more efficiently than the orthodox team plan. England, under Sir Alf Ramsey, adopted 4—2—4 and on that black day at Wembley (black if you were Scottish) when we lost 9—3 it came off spectacularly, with linkmen Johnny Haynes and Bobby Robson clicking to perfection.

The greater mobility that 4—2—4 *can* give a team depends so much on the ability of the linkmen that there is no point in adopting it if you haven't got specific players to carry it out. And it must be flexible. The four attackers must still be willing and able to come back and defend, and the four defenders to come up in support of attacks, if necessary.

As a boy I was guilty myself of trying to be a one-man band, and I know that this is a very common fault in boys' soccer. Everyone wants to be a star, to try the impossible on his own: wingers run too far with the ball and lose it; defenders dribble and leave gaps for goals; forwards would rather try wild shots at goal than pass to better-placed mates.

I suppose all boys are secretly hoping that someone will see them starring and 'discover' them. Well, in my experience there's no better way to impress anyone than playing a whole-hearted match *for your team*. Remember, what impresses other boys is not what always impresses the more adult spectator. He can tell who is playing selfishly, trying to steal the limelight, and who is doing his best by his team.

There are different ways of looking at football matches. Taking the man who runs any team as 'the expert' (in theory anyway), you have to try to *think* why certain players do the things they do. For instance, you'll often hear a crowd praise a player who has sent a beautiful long ball to an unmarked colleague.

Seldom do you hear cheers for the man who ran into the open position to make the pass possible. In my opinion the man who made the pass was doing the obvious thing in a competent way. The other man was possibly showing a touch of real inspiration.

Along with a grasp of the basic team tactics needed to enable eleven players to mould together as a team, each man must know the rules of the game. Some people may think it strange that such a controversial player as myself is anxious to increase other people's knowledge of the rules. My own experiences may be of some help to boys who are on the small side. Perhaps because I was always smaller than most boys I played against I have always gone in for a strong, determined type of play. Even now I weigh only ten stone and if I am making a challenge for the ball against a larger man I have to put that much more effort into it than a heavier man.

Often my type of player feels he is being penalised simply because he has to be that much quicker and more determined than other players if he is to be on equal terms.

I have the feeling I will always be a controversial player, if only for these reasons. I certainly hold my own failings—such as unthinking retaliation when fouled particularly badly—in no respect and while I would like to see more young players growing up with the will to win, the last thing you want to do is develop a taste for rough stuff. It makes your team less efficient, it hinders your own development and it may result in disciplinary action, which at schools level can be much more severe than in the professional game.

Play it hard—but play it clean.

F

The most misunderstood rule I find is Number 11, dealing with offside. There are men who have been watching football all their lives who still do not understand that you cannot move into an offside position *after* the ball was last played, nor if the ball was last played by an opponent (nor from a corner, throw-in, goal-kick or referee's bounce-up).

One tactic I would advise you to ban for all time from your team—the offside game. Like the Italian habit of crowding the defence, it reduces football to a negative bore—and will very probably cost your team goals in the long run. A quick move upfield by your defence to leave the opposing forwards offside will work nine times out of ten—but there will always be that tenth time when the linesman doesn't raise his flag, and there is nothing more tragic in football than the sight of a whole defence floundering halfway up the field while forwards have a clear run at goal.

I am sure nobody enjoys playing this type of football. You'll do best if you enjoy *every* moment of your soccer.

THIRTEEN

PENALTIES, CORNERS AND FREE-KICKS

Penalties

The worst penalty-kick ordeal I've seen was during a Charity Shield match between Manchester United and Everton at the beginning of the 1963–4 season. Everton's Welsh inside-left star Vernon stepped up to take the kick. On his first attempt he stopped just as he was taking the kick, our goalkeeper Dave Gaskell moving too early.

On Vernon's second attempt Gaskell made a brilliant save, but the referee saw his linesman waving the flag. Our left-back Noel Cantwell had moved into the area before the kick was actually taken—and as you will know the rules of the game make the penalty an exclusive affair between the kicker and the goalkeeper. For the third time they faced each other—and this time Roy Vernon scored.

There is always a great deal of tension surrounding a penalty kick and while few have to be taken three times, the seemingly simple business of hitting a dead ball past a goalkeeper from twelve yards can become a nerve-racking experience, at the best of times, but particularly in a big game, or when there is a lot at stake on the result of the kick.

What is the best way to take a penalty? It's a question that is often asked and I am afraid that my immediate reply may sound a bit silly. The best way to take a penalty is the way that gets the ball in the net. What I mean is—the best way for *you*. There are many different ways of approaching this vital kick, ranging from the howitzer drive that aims to take ball and goalkeeper into the net, to the 'curly' push which trickles the ball in at the foot of the post.

Older supporters of Aberdeen will remember the burly Don Emery, a massive right-back who could hit a dead ball so ferociously that many goalies who did get in the way of his shots were knocked over the line, or at least their outstretched arms were brushed aside by the sheer force of the ball. In my own team Bobby Charlton believes in taking a full-blooded bang at the ball when he steps up to the spot.

Generally you will find that the harder you hit the ball the less control you have over its direction, and apart from the one or two players who 'have a bang' I would say that most penalty-takers go for accuracy of direction first and pace afterwards.

One of the greatest penalty-takers ever seen was wee Tommy Harmer of Spurs. Not only did Harmer have a fantastic ability to kick a curving, spinning ball from the spot, but he had the knack of not making it obvious to the goalkeeper which foot he was going to use, let alone which direction the ball would take.

This brings me to the tactics goalkeepers use to try saving penalty kicks. The rule is that you cannot move until the ball has been kicked—and that does not leave you much time for a dive. Obviously the penalty-taker is going to have more success the farther he gets the ball away from the goalkeeper, so he aims to get the ball just inside the post.

Some goalkeepers take up a stance to one side of the

goal, hoping to entice the kicker to aim for the wider gap—which the goalkeeper is prepared for. Others make a guess and dive in that direction as soon as the ball moves. I suppose that more often than not a right-footed player running up to the ball in a slight curve from his left will kick the ball to the goalkeeper's right hand—this will certainly be true of younger players who have not completely mastered the art of kicking a dead ball. The goalkeeper watches the run-up and from his instinctive knowledge of how a body balances itself for a kick he makes a snap judgement. It is always a feather in a goalkeeper's cap if he saves a penalty, and if he doesn't—well, he is not blamed for missing what *should* be an almost certain goal.

The secret of the tricky penalty-taker like Tommy Harmer is to make the job easier for himself by suggesting to the goalkeeper from his run-up that the ball is going one way and then sending it the other. One of the finest examples of this was seen at Wembley Stadium in the 1963 England–Scotland match. Scotland were leading by one goal (scored by Jim Baxter) when we were awarded a penalty kick. Jim Baxter was given the job. Scotland were playing with ten men, Eric Caldow, our left-back from Rangers, having been carried off with a broken leg. Although we had been well on top of England, we had only one goal to show for our pressure. A penalty miss always gives the other team fresh heart. And the home countries' championship depended on this match. Can you imagine that many players would try *not* to catch the skipper's eye in that situation?

Not so the ice-cool Jim Baxter. He ran at the ball, did a quick double-feint and side-footed it into the net while Gordon Banks dived the wrong way.

Most teams these days have an acknowledged penalty

'king', someone who has proved that he has the temperament and the skill to convert penalty kicks. You can easily practise penalty-taking with the help of someone in goal. The ball should travel so fast that even if the goalkeeper guesses its direction directly he does not have time to leap across into its path. One tip to try out is to vary your run-up. Because we tend to kick the ball with the instep, the foot at an angle to the ground, it is natural to approach the ball from the side rather than from directly behind. The straighter the line between you, the ball and the goalkeeper as you start your approach, the less obvious it will be which side he has to dive to.

As far as the other players are concerned, the taking of a penalty kick should not be a signal for a rest. Forwards should be ready for a ball rebounding from bar or post, as the kicker cannot have a second go until another player has touched the ball. Defenders should be poised to rush in to clear a ball which the goalkeeper may have parried but not held. The penalty-taker should be ready to follow the ball, as he has a start on the other players outside the box, and many goals have been scored by an alert follow-up to penalty kicks which goalkeepers have saved only partially.

Corners

In the section on the duties of a wing-man I have dealt with the corner kick to some extent, but as this is such an important part of football it will do no harm to study general corner tactics.

First of all, the corner is an award to the attacking team and they should have the advantage. They can dictate the type of corner—out-swinger, in-swinger, short corner. With the in-swinging corner kick the ball goes out in a curve and comes back towards the goal. In some cases it is easy to tell what the winger will do— a right-footed player taking a corner on the left wing is obviously going to curl it into goal, and *vice versa* on the right. Jimmy Greaves takes many corners from the right-wing with his left foot, clipping them into goal in such a way that the goalkeeper has to wait for the ball to come to him—instead of being able to cut out the normal high cross.

The in-swinger can actually be a scoring attempt— Alex Cheyne of Aberdeen scored directly from a corner in a Hampden game with England, the first direct corner score after a change in the laws which had previously banned goals from corner kicks. The great Charlie Tully of Glasgow Celtic scored from a direct corner for Eire against England in a post-war international, and when Freddie Cox was Arsenal's right-winger he scored from direct in one of the London club's great post-war cup runs.

What the defence must do against the in-swinger is fall farther back on the goal-line than normal, a full-back at each goalpost and wing-halves close in to goal, preventing the other team from pushing the ball into the net on first bounce. A good winger will be able to vary from out-swingers to in-swingers without changing his feet, but getting the in-swinger by using the outside of his foot instead of the instep.

For defence against the short corner—which was used particularly cleverly by Spurs in their recent years of success—a wing-half should go out to mark the second man. The idea is that the winger passes a short ball to a colleague, receives a quick return pass which leaves him clear of the defender and allows him to bring the ball close to goal. This can be deadly against a static defence which stands rooted to the positions taken up for an orthodox corner: as soon as it is obvious that a short corner is being taken the defence must realign itself, the winger falling back to help his wing-half mark the two attackers.

Generally, while the attack has the advantage in deciding what kind of corner they are taking, the defence should come off best at a corner: the defender needs to position himself to get his head to the ball and send it out of the goal area, whereas the forwards must try to position themselves to head towards a comparatively small target.

Also, there's the goalkeeper, who ninety-nine times out of a hundred should be able to cut out the high ball across goal. Wingers will get round this by dropping the ball farther out from the goal-line than the goalie finds it safe to go, or by sending a very high ball right over the goal area to the opposite winger. This can be a most effective move and the attacking team should always have someone, winger, inside-man or wing-half, who lies on the other side of the main body of players ready for the ball that everyone else misses. The defence should guard against this by marking this space. It is debatable whether a centre-half or other tallish defender should go up to help his forwards head goals from corner kicks. I know that Jackie Charlton of Leeds and Mike England of Spurs do this a lot, bringing their extra inches into play in the crowded goalmouth.

They do get goals this way, but remember that they are part of teams which have practised tactics together for years and whenever they go up they leave someone else behind to cover their positions. Apart from the really spectacular headers of a ball, like Tommy Lawton, Dixie Dean and Jimmy McGrory (former Glasgow Celtic manager), and today's Ron Davies of Southampton, few players have the leaping ability necessary to outjump the goalkeeper—who, after all, can jump just as high and still get extra reach with his hands.

In the 1964 Scotland–England game at Hampden we won by one goal, scored by Alan Gilzean. It was magnificent goal, scored by one of the finest headers of a ball in the country. But I think there was some truth in what Sir Alf Ramsey, England team manager, said after the game—that in top-class football there should be very few, if any, goals scored by forwards heading in direct from a corner cross. I think that corners offer a great chance for new tactical thinking in football—with forwards finding new ways to use the advantage a corner gives them, and defences having to find new ways of combating them—as they fairly quickly learned to do with the short corner.

In the meantime it is important for you to practise the art of kicking corners—until you can drop the ball on any precise spot. There is something awful about the sight of a winger who tamely puts the ball past the line from a corner kick. I know—it's happened to me.

Free-kicks

Until a few years ago a free-kick anywhere on the field was the signal for a hold-up in the game while the kicker placed the ball and went back for his run, while the other players took up position for a long ball.

Nowadays, in midfield at least, this has changed: most teams prefer to get the ball moving again as quickly as possible, and, indeed, many referees find they have to blow for the kick to be taken again because the ball never actually stopped moving. We find today little advantage in an elaborate free-kick, which gives a defence time to take up position and whose only advantage is to gain ground. As football has changed from the idea of making distance by use of the big kick to the principle of retaining possession of the ball by shorter passes, the free-kick has importance only in that it gives you a chance to pass to a colleague.

However, a free-kick just outside the penalty area represents a tactical challenge to defence and attack alike. The commonest means of defence is the line of players, shoulder-to-shoulder, blocking the view the kicker has of goal.

I have seen teams lining up in this way, apparently unaware of the fact that a solid line can be just as dangerous as no line at all. The reason is that a solid line effectively blocks your goalkeeper's view of what is happening: a lob over the line can catch him unprepared and so can a shot which happens to find a way through the mass of bodies immediately in front of him.

When you are forming this line, generally of four or five players, place it so that it covers the far post and half the goal, with the goalkeeper covering the rest. The kicker then has little to aim at.

In fact, the idea of blasting a goal from one of these free-kicks is going out of fashion. More common now is for the attack to try to trick the defence. Two or even three players line up as though they are going to take the kick. They all run, one jumps over the ball, another runs to one side and the third either tries a shot through the gaps which the feint has caused or a quick pass to a forward who is in a position to move round the line of defenders.

The wall was designed to block the slam-bang shot at goal and although this has gone out of fashion slightly, the wall is still necessary, for many players would give themselves a good chance of beating a goalkeeper with a clear kick at goal from just outside the penalty area. What a defence must practise is the correct positioning of the wall, and the marking of other opposing forwards by their own attack.

Then again, the great Didi of Brazil could swerve the ball round the wall in a half-circle, so that it curled into goal by the far post, the side the goalkeeper is not covering. Other players will try to float one over the wall, aiming to get the ball to drop in just under the bar.

I feel that all of these different tactics can be effective —*if* they can be varied from time to time, so that the defence is never sure what is going to happen. You can practise them with your own team, defence against attack, until you achieve an understanding with each other on what you are going to do in any given set of circumstances, yet without ever getting so rigid in your approach that you cannot see and take advantage of unexpected openings and chances. Tactics are essential —but they are for your use, not your master.

FOURTEEN

CAPTAINCY, DISCIPLINE AND REFEREES

When Noel Cantwell, Manchester United's skipper, went out of the team through injury in the 1963–4 season Sir Matt Busby made me team captain. I took the job thinking there was really nothing to it. I'd always regarded the captain of a league side as the man who tossed up and did little else.

I know one thing that being captain did for me. Before I was given the job I had been in trouble with referees fairly frequently, but in the time I was captain I was in trouble a lot less, the responsibility of knowing that I was captain making me a lot more aware of the need to set an example on the field.

In a First Division side the duties of a team captain are confined largely to bringing a personal influence to bear on the team rather than telling them how to play the game, because most of the team are experienced professionals; tactics have been worked out in the week before each game and even in cases of injury it has already been decided by the manager what positional reshuffles will take place.

Indeed, some teams think so little of the captain's role that he is asked simply to toss up and no more. To my mind this is bad. A good captain is the leader of the side and by example and by what he says, on and off the field, he can do a great deal to help his team. In my case this was an easy part of the job, because I used to keep up a constant flow of advice to my team-mates and as captain I suppose they tended to listen to me just a little bit. You would get a fair idea of what other part a good captain can play watching Manchester United training.

Noel Cantwell, now Coventry's manager, used to take the defence, first team and reserves and youngsters to one part of the training ground. There he put them through their paces. He took our goalkeeper who was David Gaskell to the small-size training nets and made him kneel on the goal-line. Then Noel threw the ball at the net. Dave had to keep leaping up off his knees to save and you could hear Noel's Irish voice prodding him to greater efforts. He put two full-backs in the large goals and the whole defence lobbed in ball after ball which they had to head off the line. Then he put one man in goal, one at centre-half and another at centre-forward and had balls crossed from either wing, to give them practice at headed clearances.

Everybody went through these routines, first-team stars and boys alike, with Noel exhorting them on in his strong brogue. He genuinely took an interest in each player's progress, which gave everyone the idea that they were working just as much to help their own development as putting in the required amount of training.

In league football the captain is usually a defender, because that gives him the best view of the game. I think that one of the wing-halves is best placed to lead the side because they are more in the game than anyone.

He is not necessarily the best player in the side—his personality matters more in a professional side than his playing ability and you imagine that anyone in a league side has enough skill to justify his leadership of the team.

However, there are bad captains in professional football: in my opinion the most common are those who never say a word on the field and who might as well not be there at all as far as showing any leadership qualities.

There is a great deal of difference between the best captain for a professional side and for an amateur or boys' team. The ability to talk sense about the game does not impress youngsters greatly if there is not a good deal of evidence to show that the person who is talking can play as well and for this reason I think that all young teams should be captained by the best player in the side. All boys tend to hero-worship someone and they will respect the words of the star player whereas they might ignore advice from anyone else.

What does a captain do? He tosses up for ends and even here he can help his side a great deal. In league football we generally have no great preference for kicking with or against the wind in the first half. If anything I prefer playing against the wind because the ball does not run away from you all the time. I have often heard players say at half-time in the dressing-room that 'things will be better this half, we're kicking against the wind'. Naturally we have stronger bodies than young boys and we can cope with a strong head-wind. My advice to young captains is to play with the wind in the first half if they win the toss. They will have the help of the wind when they are still fresh and there is always the very likely chance, in our climate, of a gale dying down by the second half. Of course, a team that can naturally keep the ball on the ground, where the wind has least effect, will always do better than opponents who bash the ball about in the air.

Another part of the captain's duties occurs when there is an injury. He the one who says what happens. There are basic rules which you might follow for injuries. First, always have a player already selected for playing in goal if the goalkeeper has to go off the field. This player should have done a bit of practice between the sticks, and when he puts on the jersey the other ten men do not feel that they have a wide open goal behind them. The main thing about covering the other positions is to know in advance the capabilities and the preferences of the other players in your team.

When Scotland played England at Wembley in 1963 our left-back, Eric Caldow of Rangers, was carried off with a broken leg after a collision with Bobby Smith. It is usual for the wing-half to fall back in this case, but that would have meant that Scotland would lose the invaluable work of Jim Baxter of Rangers in midfield and attack, so Davie Wilson, the Rangers' outside-left, was pulled back to left-back. Remember there were no substitutions then. Not only did he play a fantastically good game in defence, but Baxter was able to stay on in attack. The wisdom of this decision was shown when Jim scored the two goals (one a penalty) which gave us victory. If he had been restricted to the defensive role of full-back we would probably not have got those goals— and England would have been able to keep stronger pressure on our goal.

One of the more arguable decisions is when a player is injured but is still able to limp along fairly well. The old idea was to put him on the wing or at centre forward. This was before the substitution rule came into effect, whereby the injured player could be replaced by a fit one thus not reducing the team's efficiency unfairly.

It is advisable however to make sure that the injury is

95

serious enough to need a substitute, because once made, the decision cannot be revoked and the injured player return. If another player hurts himself and has to go off, then the team is unnecessarily down to ten men again.

The best thing to do if a player gets injured is to take him to the touchline for treatment and if after two or three minutes he has recovered, he can return and nothing is lost and your substitute can be held back until really needed.

One thing that is important when the injured player is temporarily off the field, do not allow your defence to be weakened. If he is a defender, then bring one of the forwards back to fill his place until he is fit again.

As I told you before, the responsibility of being captain of Manchester United during the absence of Noel Cantwell seemed to keep me out of trouble with referees, and there is a great deal a captain can do to improve the behaviour and discipline of his team. While not trying to be the big boss (and in most sides the manager has already made most of the important decisions in advance) he should be ready to have a word with any player who seems to be losing his temper or misbehaving in any way.

As far as behaviour on the field is concerned, the sensible thing to bear in mind is that a breach of the rules which leads to a player being sent off is a serious handicap to the team. I have been as guilty as most of losing my temper on the field: I think I have gone a long way to curing this simply because it was brought home to me that the only effect it was having was to harm the side's chances.

If the captain of a team is always in trouble, going in for rough stuff or continually arguing with the referee,

25 *Corners* Using his left foot to take a corner from the right wing, Denis approaches the ball from behind the bye-line to hit an in-swinging corner. Note that for in-swingers the ball is placed on the bye-line.

26 *Throw-ins* Feet apart, Denis arches his whole body backwards to get maximum distance for his throw-in. The ball must come from behind the player's head, and both feet must be on the ground.

27 *Crossing the ball* Alan Hinton, the Derby winger, is perfectly balanced with his left foot beside the ball, body bent forwards a little and both eyes on the ball.

28 (Left) *Crossing the ball* Denis crosses, showing how the foot comes in contact with the bottom half of the ball, giving an up and under effect. The West Bromwich left-half uses his left leg as a shield in an attempt to block the cross.

his team-mates will tend to follow his example.

In the heat of the moment it is understandable appealing to the referee about what you imagine are wrong decisions. However, it is not only useless (did you ever hear of a referee changing his mind because the players argued?) but stupid as well, for nothing is more likely to put people off football than the sight of a crowd of players pushing and shoving round the referee. As the critics say, it does generally look very childish.

However, theory is often different from reality and in this case I am on the side of the players who appeal. Of course, it does no good—I know that when I raise my arms in horror at some offside decision—but it is a sign that the player concerned is whole-heartedly involved in the game. If you have been striving with all your energy it is only understandable that you are visibly disappointed when you are pulled up. Players with heart will go making noisy appeals despite all the correct behaviour they are taught and I shall be one of them.

This brings me to relations with referees. Here I must be on the side of the rules. I have known good referees, terrible referees and one or two brilliant referees, but in all cases it is the player's duty to follow the rules and keep his opinion of the man in charge to himself. Certainly no young player should ever allow himself to be involved with infringements of the rules which lead to disciplinary action on the field.

In a now infamous international match at Hampden Park in the 1963–4 season Scotland were beating Austria 4—0 when the game began to deteriorate to a depth I have never before seen on a football field. The Austrian team seemed to have given up playing football altogether—they made no attempt to tackle or intercept, and gradually the game became less like football

G

and more like all-in wrestling. To everybody's surprise the referee ran off the field before the end, and after we had stood around for a few minutes we were told he had abandoned the game.

In this case I can feel that no blame attached itself to D. Law, Esquire, although I have not always been so lucky. In my time I have been warned ('Don't do that again or else,' the ref generally says), had my name taken (of course they know your name but you still go through the business of saying 'Law' when the black book is produced) and sent off.

I am not proud of any of these incidents. I think that in some young teams there is a feeling that getting into this kind of trouble makes you out to be a big tough guy: my advice is to regard the kind of player who continually gets in trouble as a laughing-stock. He does his own team no good and he does himself no good. *Anybody* can play this game dirtily, for there is no skill in kicking and punching. I know that it happens in league football—perhaps more than it should—but in the tension of big professional matches there may be some excuse for a player to lose his head. There is none in youth or amateur football. If you find that you are being frequently tackled unfairly or fouled by an opponent the best thing is to draw the attention of the referee: if he is any good at all—and most referees in junior soccer are doing the job because they love the game—he will stamp down on the offender. If he does nothing your only course is to avoid getting in that situation again. Learning how to evade—rather than retaliate—is a valuable lesson in anybody's soccer apprenticeship.

I will end this part about referees with the comment that in professional soccer the best referees in the world, in my opinion, are Scottish, with English whistlers a good second and the rest of the world nowhere. I have had my ups and downs with referees, more than I care to remember. Only now do I think that age—and the effects of being captain—helped me calm down my naturally quick impulses. You will do yourself a great service if you learn the same lesson sooner than I did.

FIFTEEN

TAKING YOUR CHANCES

I was a very excited youngster when I ran on to the field at Ninian Park, Cardiff, for my very first international match. The date was 18th October 1958, and like any teenager who is picked to play for his country I was nervous about my chances of proving I was good enough.

Scotland scored three goals to beat Wales that day. Probably because it was such an important game for me I remember them all vividly—and the lesson that the three goals taught me is valid for any football player.

A goal is scored by getting the ball over the line. It doesn't matter *how* you put the ball in the net. It doesn't matter *who* scores as long as it is a member of your side. Goals count and it is every player's duty to remember always that his job is to get the ball in the other team's net.

I scored a goal in that first international match—and it was one of the flukiest scores I have ever seen in a football game. We were in the second half when David Herd crossed the ball from the right-wing. I had been trying to make up for my inexperience by putting every ounce of energy I possessed into the game and I was in position to go for the cross. I went for the ball, challenging the Welsh left-half and skipper, Dave Bowen, then of Arsenal and now the Welsh Manager. Dave got there first. His clearance hit my head and I stood, as amazed as everyone else, as the ball soared in an arc past goalkeeper Jack Kelsey. It crossed the line and spun back into his arms. I had scored a goal!

Now I don't imagine my fluky first international goal will ever be thought of very highly by students of the game, but there is a lesson to be learned. Fluke or not, it would not have happened if I had not been going in for the ball when Dave Bowen tried to clear it. I was in the right position—and that is three-quarters of the battle when it comes to seizing chances.

The other two goals Scotland scored that day were almost textbook models of how to do it correctly, and are worth recalling. The first came after about thirty minutes of play. I won the ball in midfield and saw Jackie Henderson unmarked on the left-wing. I gave him a pass. He took the ball down the wing with his usual speed and crossed a perfect ball to Graham Leggatt, who headed the goal. From midfield to goal in two moves—the direct method.

Our third was more involved—but still done with the kind of simple, straightforward thinking that produces results. As Tommy Docherty hit a free-kick to our right-back, John Grant, I began running from the centre circle towards the Welsh goal. Grant saw me running and when I'd covered about thirty-five yards he sent a long ball through the Welsh defence. I saw Dave Mackay also running forward and I nodded the ball, first-time, in his path. He swept it straight to Bobby Collins (then Everton), and Bobby scored our third.

The variety of goals that can be scored is, you'll see from just that one game, immense. In fact, when you think of all the possible moves in a game you may come to the conclusion that no two goals are ever exactly the same. However, there are some general rules about seizing goal chances which you would be well advised to follow.

It is a fact, for instance, that most goals come from inside the penalty area. Only occasionally do long shots reach the net and while there is always a temptation to try to blast one in from thirty yards, you will do better for your team by working to bring the ball closer in where someone else will probably be in a better position to score.

Another hard-and-fast rule is—you can never shoot *too* low. By the very balance of the human body, most kicks will produce a ball that rises, so the thing to practise in shooting is to keep the ball as low as possible. Not only does this increase your chances of being on target, but it also makes the goalkeeper's job more difficult, as diving to a ground ball takes longer than jumping to a high ball.

A third rule is to act as quickly as possible when a scoring chance comes along. The penalty area is no place to dally around in, bringing the ball to your favourite foot or trying to beat another man to get into a better position. If the ball comes to you chest high within striking distance of the goal the best move is to try to hook it in first time rather than breast it down first.

One of the greatest goal-scorers of modern football is Jimmy Greaves. What impresses every one—and this includes professional players as well—about Jimmy is his fantastic ability to seize on the slightest chance near goal and get the ball in the net. Quite apart from his razor-edged reflexes, which give Jimmy that little extra bit of time at moments when other players are taking time to think what they will do next, a great deal of the Greaves success near goal is due to his attitude of mind. Being give a chance—or, more often, half a chance—near goal does not send him into a panicky excitement as happens with many players, the kind who seem to go to pieces within sight of goal and either miss the ball altogether or blast it a mile over the bar.

Few people will ever get to the Greaves standard but you can practice the art of snapping up short-distance goals (kicking first time against a wall is one way) until you have confidence that you can repeat the performance in an actual game.

Another player who has a knack of scoring goals is Joe Baker, with whom I spent a season in Italy. Joe's knack is slightly different from Jimmy Greaves': he has the ability to turn—on a sixpence, as they say—and fire in medium-range shots which beat goalkeepers because of the speed he gets the shot in and the pace of the ball.

With Greaves you have the art of the close-in goal, where speed of action is all-important (you shouldn't really need to think about what you are doing), and the ball is placed rather than rammed into the net.

With Baker you have the epitome of the more orthodox goal, the twelve- or fifteen-yard shot which has both direction and power to pass the goalkeeper.

A third common source of goals is the run and shot, where one player takes the ball from midfield and finishes his run with a goal-scoring attempt. Many players fumble this chance because the run tires them out and by the time they are within shooting distance they are ready to collapse. This is worth practising—on your own if necessary—making long runs followed by shots at goal.

These are some of the basic rules and tips for taking goal chances, but this is a complicated subject—one of the most varied of all the arts of football, and there are many other ways in which goals can be scored. These can be put down to 'opportunism' rather than to any particular tactical plan. The first thing about opportunism—sometimes called poaching, making it sound, somehow, unfair, which is absolute nonsense—is that you have to be in position to take your opportunities. The opportunist *never* gives up.

In the 1962–3 season Manchester United were playing Southampton in the semi-final of the F.A. Cup at Villa Park when I got the winning goal—which could only be credited to my belief that the place to score goals is right in there at your opponent's goal when the chance arises.

Again it was David Herd who crossed the ball from the right. This time I headed it at very short range. Southampton's goalkeeper Reynolds pushed the ball out. I had followed up my header and as the ball fell stabbed it into the net—standing almost face to face with Reynolds!

While I don't want to appear as though I am the only player in the country who scores this kind of goal, it is easier for me to explain why I do certain things rather than try to read the thoughts of other players, and one goal that United scored in a league game with Notts Forest may show you that it is possible to score goals without even touching the ball.

Albert Quixall centred the ball from the right-wing. The ball was not travelling particularly fast but I could see that it was going towards goal. Three Nottingham defenders were obviously waiting for me to fasten on to the ball. Instead, at the last moment, I let it go on—into the net.

I am sure that your mental attitude is one of the keys

to success near goal. One of the most fantastic goal-scoring sprees of modern football was by the late Johnny Summers of Charlton Athletic in 1957. Summers was a one-foot player—he rarely used his right foot for anything but standing on. With half an hour to go in a league match at the Valley, Huddersfield were beating Charlton 5—1, and Charlton were a man down through injury.

In the next eighteen minutes Summers scored four goals—all with his 'wrong' foot. The final score was 7—6 for Charlton. Was it because his team seemed so hopelessly beaten that *anything* was worth trying that made Summers so deadly with his right foot that day? That may be the reason, but there is also the factor that happens to every player at some time or another—the day he can do nothing wrong.

In my case an outstanding example of this was a cup-tie in 1961 when I was with Manchester City. We were playing Luton Town on a muddy pitch and after nineteen minutes were two goals down. In the next quarter of an hour I scored a hat-trick—my very first in league football. Now this may help prove my point about your mental attitude being all-important: having seen how easily goals were coming I decided to keep trying. In the second half I scored another three!

Six goals in one game! Until that match I had always thought of myself as an also-ran as a goal-scorer. Today I reckon that I've as good a chance as anybody of getting the ball in the net and I think this game probably set me on the right mental attitude. The ironic thing is that none of my six goals meant anything—the game was abandoned because of the mud. And Luton won the replay. It's goals that count—but not the six I got on my best-ever scoring performance.

By the way, a team of psychiatrists did a series of tests on goal-scoring, using West Bromwich Albion and Manchester United players as guinea-pigs. They found that the younger and less skilful a player was, the farther away from goal he would try to shoot.

They analysed films of two Cup Finals and found that out of forty-four shots from *inside* the penalty area, thirteen produced goals. Of thirty-two shots from outside the area only one brought a goal.

I'm no psychiatrist but it seems to prove what I said was right—the nearer to goal you are, the better your chance of scoring. It's up to you to be in the right place.

SIXTEEN

TRAINING AND INJURIES

The point of training is to make you fit. The point of being fit is to enable you to play football. That seems obvious, but there is another good reason for making yourself really fit, and that is to avoid injuries.

Injuries and training are very closely linked together in modern football—certainly at the professional level—and I don't think you would be wasting your time to think about the possibility that one Saturday afternoon you may hurt yourself playing soccer. While I do not want to sound like some grand old man who is lecturing you on the game, I do think I should say that there is a great difference between football played among youngsters and the game at the top.

For instance, let me put it this way: as boys, everybody plays the game as hard as possible, sometimes two games in a day, and yet the number of times somebody gets carried off or hurt is very small compared with the injuries you hear about among professionals. I have heard some spectators blame this on the professionals—as though we were some kind of temperamental prima donnas, so frightened of being hurt that we lie down at the first opportunity.

The difference between the boy who plays football and the adult professional is something similar to the difference between the baby who falls on the ground and the grown man. Babies have been known to fall three storeys down into rock-hard pavements and suffer only bruises. Grown-ups have been known to break their backs falling ten feet. The reason is simple—the younger you are, the softer are your bones. The baby doesn't know it is falling, it doesn't tense up—and in consequence it comes through these experiences comparatively unhurt.

The older you get, the more brittle your bones become. And more and more, as you grow older becomes the need to train your body for a game of football. There is also a difference in the way a professional plays the game. He does not—as all young players do—throw himself into every second of the game as though his life depended upon it. He knows when to save his energy, when to take the easy way out.

The younger you are, the more energy you are liable to cram into every minute you are on the field. But—and it is a very big but—the professional is playing the game much more seriously: situations crop up in every game when he knows that he has to go in, regardless of the risk to himself. Nobody blames a boy for evading a difficult situation which might have caused an injury, but the professional is being paid to play football, and if he is so worried about the danger of physical contact that he holds back he won't stay at the top very long.

I think that anybody who is continually conscious of the injury risk in playing football should forget about taking up the game as a living. Broken legs, for example, are something we all have to take as a normal risk: the number of schoolboys who break a leg is very small indeed.

The most common injury any youngster stands a

chance of receiving in a game of football is a cut. What with badly fixed studs and pitches with stones, cuts and bruises are fairly common in juvenile football.

I was often cut on the legs as a youngster (even today my legs are normally fairly heavily bruised, but for different reasons). I used to shrug them off. But I know now that this is dangerous. All cuts can be a menace. There are germs in any soil which can cause serious harm to the human body, and my advice is to treat any scratch or cut immediately by getting it cleaned out, disinfected and bandaged. Many players have suffered a great deal from ignoring simple lacerations, and some have been known to lose a leg through the poison which may spread from an untreated cut. I know it may feel brave and manly to shrug them off as 'just a scratch', but you possibly are doing yourself a lot of harm.

It is well known in football that goalkeepers suffer most injuries—and that the knee is the most easily affected part of the body. If you skin your knees make sure they are washed thoroughly.

The only other injury—if it can be called that—which might affect you is the very common attack of blisters on the feet at the beginning of every season. I soak mine in chemicals before every new season to harden them. If you don't go this far you should make sure at least that there are no nails sticking up through the soles of your boots. On hard dry grounds a protruding nail can harm your feet very seriously.

I don't think that a pulled muscle is a very general complaint among healthy young players, yet it seems to affect lots of professionals—whom you might think should be trained so well they wouldn't suffer from that sort of thing.

The fact is—every footballer needs some kind of regular work-out to keep his body in trim. As it happens, I need very little training. When I went to Italy, Torino put me through a rigorous medical. My pulse was taken, then I was put through thirty minutes of the most strenuous gymnastic and athletic activity. Then they took my pulse again—and the rate had hardly changed. I have a very slow heart-beat.

I would not advise you to count on the same natural blessing. My advice is to think of football as a game in which fit players have a decided advantage. Boys do not have weight troubles—their normal activity keeps them supple, but the more speed and stamina you have, the more you will enjoy the game. And that, surely, is the main consideration.

If you want to go in for physical training, the parts that can do with most development are the legs and the chest. Strong thighs give you power for running and kicking and you can always strengthen your thighs by full knee-bending (heels off the ground), carrying a weight on your shoulders.

The larger your chest becomes, the more room there is for your lungs to expand, giving you larger supplies of oxygen. Stomach and chest muscles can be exercised by lying flat on your back, legs together, raising them into the air until you can see your toes without raising your head.

Of course, once you get to the top, things like diet come into your training—before a game I usually have steak or fish, giving myself at least two hours between the meal and the kick-off.

Basically, I would say that any boy should concentrate on playing with a ball as his real training. The earlier you get to bed the better. Anything that keeps you running, walking and breathing deeply is good for your body.

Leave the more involved type of training until you are older. It's bad enough then without causing yourself unnecessary suffering.

SEVENTEEN

CAN YOU WATCH AND LEARN?

In the 1963–4 season Manchester United were playing Southampton in the F.A. Cup. I was not in the team, having been suspended. I watched most of the first half. We were down 2—0. I stayed in the dressing-room in the second half, physically unable to watch the rest of the match.

I could hear the roars of the crowd, but had no way of telling whether we were scoring or Southampton were piling on even more goals. I paced up and down our dressing-room, no more able to watch the rest of the game than fly in the air.

Of course, *you* can learn something by watching football. The strange fact is—*I* cannot. If I am not in the Manchester team I find that I am too nervous to watch the boys playing. I once travelled to Chelsea—and never even saw the pitch.

And if Manchester United are not playing then I have no desire to watch *any* game of football. I'm unable to explain this clearly, even to myself, but the fact is that if the two greatest teams in the world were playing for the world championship half a mile away from my home I would probably not make the effort to see them.

Perhaps I am too restless to sit and watch other men playing football. Perhaps it has something to do with the fact that as a boy I never got into the habit of watching professional football on Saturday afternoons.

29 Stoke and England goalkeeper Gordon Banks makes a courageous save from Colin Suggett.

30 (Above) *Goalkeeping* Gary Sprake of Leeds foils a determined Manchester United attack.

31 (Below) *Role of centre-half* The centre-half or sweeper as he is more commonly known is the kingpin of the defence. Here Ian Ure now with Manchester United breaks up a Stoke challenge by heading clear.

As a boy in Aberdeen I rarely went to see Aberdeen playing, the only occasions being big matches with teams like Glasgow Rangers. In fact, if you ask me if I ever learned anything watching league football I must answer that the only things I remember about the games I did see at Pittodrie (Aberdeen's ground) were the great long legs of the famous Rangers and Scotland captain George Young and the fantastic speed of Willie Waddell, the Rangers outside-right who became their manager later. You could hardly base a professional career on *that*, could you?

However, I do know of one or two professional players who say they modelled themselves as boys on star players. I will not mention any names, because, frankly, I do not believe them. They may *think* they copied someone else, but it is virtually impossible for one footballer to copy the style of another: differences in weight, physique and mental approach to the game must be taken into account.

It is natural for all boys to worship a hero and sometimes they confuse hero-worship with playing style. I don't think there's any harm in a youngster imagining that he's playing football the way Jimmy Greaves or Bobby Moore plays it, but I cannot see this doing any positive good to his football.

What I want to stress to all young players is the need to *think* about football. And if you know what it is possible to learn from watching a league match then you will not be wasting your Saturday afternoon.

The more you think about the game, the more obvious it will be to you that the star you admire most is not always the player you can learn most from. In fact, to take the sensible viewpoint, the star is often a little bit of a freak—and trying to copy him is a waste of time.

H   113

No, what you can learn from watching is something different. First of all, you can soak in a set of playing standards towards which you can practise. Young defenders watching good-class league soccer should understand the practical demonstration they will get of the need to use the ball constructively, rather than boot it up the field regardless.

You can see certain tricks being put into operation—and having seen them done correctly, go away and practise them yourself.

One move spread through football in this country today was introduced by international players after games against the South Americans. This is running on to a ball in such a way that your body shields it from the man who is challenging you. Instead of taking the shortest possible route to the ball from where you are standing, you try to move on to it in a direction which puts you between the ball and the nearest defender. This is a move which can best be picked up by watching rather than by theoretical lessons.

But to appreciate the value of what you are seeing you must be prepared to watch a game of football not so much from the idea of cheering on your home team but with the attitude that you are on the terracing to learn something. You must *think*.

If you don't believe me, let me tell you about a young First Division player I know. In some ways he is a tragedy in himself, because he has enough natural attributes to make him one of the greatest stars this country has ever seen. On his day he is dazzling. But—because he is purely a natural player who never even attempts to think about the game—his day comes only on one or two games in every five he plays. If the ball

114

doesn't run right for him he has no mental foundations on which can remedy his bad luck.

Thirty years ago he might have been a star, because soccer was more instinctive in those days and more was left to the individual player to work out his own approach to the game. Today soccer is becoming more and more scientific: sheer ball control and speed are not enough unless you have a brain to back them up.

Not having watched much soccer from the terracings I am not, perhaps, the best person to tell you where to stand in a ground for the best view for learning purposes. However, I would say that the more different angles you watch from the better. Tactics are best seen from a higher, midfield position on the terraces—you can watch the flow of the game and the teamwork of both sets of players from there.

Aspiring goalkeepers should be able to learn something from standing immediately behind the goal so that they get as near to the goalkeeper's viewpoint as possible.

You can study the position he takes up for the various attacks on the goal that he has to meet and when forwards are running in on goal you should be able to see what angle he moves out at to give his goal the maximum cover. The rule is—the farther away from the players you are, the more overall the picture you will get of general team movements. The nearer you are the more you will appreciate the actual physical actions required to carry out individual moves.

Although I have said that I dislike watching football, that does not mean that I am so big-headed I think there's nothing more for me to learn. I learn something new in every game I play. The moment you stop learning about this game you are as good as finished. Twice a week at Manchester United we have a general discussion about our last game. The Boss tells us, individually and collectively, what we did wrong, what weaknesses showed up in our teamwork and what we should try to improve in our next game. In his calm, tactful and wise way he guides us to a better understanding of what the game is all about—and from teenage apprentices to first-team international stars there isn't one member of the playing staff who thinks he knows enough about the game to ignore The Boss's words.

It's not always a new lesson that we have to learn, either. Some of the simplest basic rules of the game have to be continually dinned into your head. For instance, I hung my head in a game with Sheffield United at Old Trafford in April 1963. We were perilously near the bottom of the table and we needed every point we could gather. At a crucial stage of the game David Herd swung across a fine centre from which I ordinarily would have expected to score.

However, I thought I was in an offside position and forgetting the most basic of all rules—play to the whistle—I didn't try to score but merely tapped the ball tamely towards goal and waited for the referee to stop play.

The whistle never came. The Blades moved straight to the other end and scored. The game was a 1—1 draw —but if I had played to the whistle we would almost certainly have won. Now if you had been watching that game you might have come to the conclusion from seeing this happen that it was 'just one of those things': professional footballers often *seem* to take a rather casual attitude to incidents which drive fans mad. Believe me, it was not 'one of those things'—it was a stupid error of judgement for which I could have kicked myself. Footballers feel these things—probably a great deal more deeply than the crowd which yells at them—but we are trained to get on with the game. The time to get worked up about your mistakes is later on when you have a chance to decide exactly where you went wrong and why.

All in all, I would say that any young player who is willing to think about the game should be able to learn something from watching football—whether it's the Cup Final or a public-park scratch game. But to be able to put the lessons he's learned into effect he must practise his own skills by playing the game and by working on his own. Nobody ever became a great player by watching other great players. If that was possible we would have more stars than spectators.

EIGHTEEN

MAGIC MOMENTS

I have a dream that occurs frequently during every week of the football season—especially on Friday night before a big game. In this dream I play the most wonderful game of my life. I make perfect passes which always come off, I am always in the right position—and I end up scoring at least five goals.

I don't mind admitting that I often have this dream while I am still awake, for no matter how many games I play, or how many seasons I put behind me, I still have a fantastic optimism about the next match. It may surprise you—but as soon as a game is finished it is virtually forgotten as far as I am concerned. My philosophy is—you get nowhere thinking about last year's matches (except, of course, as I have said, in learning something about the game).

However, there have been magic moments in my career which I have not forgotten. I will tell you about some of them, not so much from a desire to brag about my moments of glory, but to show you the type of achievement which a professional footballer can be proud of—and to illustrate some of the theoretical points I have been making.

I think the greatest single moment was the goal I scored in the 1963 Cup Final. United had been having a poor league season, and our team of talent had shown few signs of clicking together. Some people were surprised we had reached the final at all, for our cup wins up to Wembley had not exactly been totally convincing. On the other hand, Leicester City were a closely knit team with a very good record: the critics thought that their brilliantly solid teamwork would carry them through against the more erratic, if slightly more star-studded, United. Leicester had been at Wembley not long before, losing to Spurs when the London team won the double. I think there was a feeling that a team which lost one year in the final would be bound by law of averages to win on its second appearance.

My own view was that the first team to score would win the game. Our plan was to try to keep possession of the ball and make Leicester do the running. In the opening stages there was nothing much to choose between us, although our teamwork seemed to be clicking much more efficiently than it had all season. After twenty-nine minutes Bobby Charlton shot and Gordon Banks smothered the ball. As he came forward, our right-half, Pat Crerand, sized up the situation—Banks was going to throw the ball to Leicester's inside-left Davie Gibson. As Pat says, you can tell when a man wants the ball by the way he runs, and even as Banks was drawing back his arm to throw to Gibson, Pat started running in anticipation of an interception. (Lesson 1—Pat Crerand was alive to everything happening—just because the goalkeeper had saved he did not fall back to see what Leicester would do next.)

Pat moved past one Leicester player and gathered the ball before it could reach Gibson. I could see that Pat was moving forward in the inside-left position and that he had no chance of scoring. I knew he would have to pass, so I started running forward into the penalty area on his right (Lesson 2—position yourself for the pass).

At the same time, Pat told me later, he was thinking to himself that a shot would be hopeless. He spotted me running on his right, and, as the Leicester full-back Norman made to tackle, Pat swung the ball across to me. It came at me about six inches off the ground, travelling harder than I expected. Normally I would have tried a left-foot shot, but the Leicester defenders were crowding me on that side. First I had to stop the ball. A fraction mistiming here and it would have bounced away from my feet at the speed it was moving. I pulled it down (Lesson 3—there was no time to think or have a second chance—this is where the hours of practice pay off) and swung away from the goal, turning in a circle so that I swivelled round again with the ball at my right foot, facing a gap in the defence. As soon as I saw goal I took a swipe at the ball.

I had no idea where the goalkeeper was, and I couldn't tell you what part of my foot actually connected with the ball. I scored, and my prophecy came true—the first team to score won the cup. It all happened a lot faster than the time it has taken you to read about it, and this is the fourth lesson to be learned: when your big chance comes are you confident that you've done enough work to be able to snatch it, as I was lucky enough to do at Wembley? There was no time to start thinking about what to do next—there never is in the penalty area. Instant action is what counts, and the fact that you have worked and sweated perfecting your game to ensure that your actions pay off.

My first game for Scotland, against Wales at Ninian Park, Cardiff, was another magic moment—especially when I scored a goal, fluky as it was (see Chapter 15). Some people have the idea that to a professional footballer playing for one team is very much like playing for another and that only spectators get emotional about international matches and other vital games. This is far from true. Any player with a future in the game soon finds that no matter what team he is playing for, he wants that team to win. This is true of transferred players who occasionally find themelves playing against their old club a week later. A footballer thinks this way: this club thinks enough of me to have bought me, I owe them my best.

In youth football there is a great deal of changing around. Many boys, as I did, play two games on a Saturday, one for the school in the morning and another for a youth club or juvenile team in the afternoon. Generally the desire to be on the winning side is enough to ensure whole-hearted endeavour and I would say that if you find yourself playing half-heartedly for a side whose success or failure doesn't bother you either way you should find a new team to play with. The half-hearted footballer is nobody's friend and his own worst enemy.

I suppose another of my magic moments was running on to the field with Huddersfield at Meadow Lane. It was Christmas Eve, 1956, our opponents were Notts County and I was sixteen.

My wing partner, Kevin McHale, was seventeen. I was the youngest player to have represented Huddersfield and we were the youngest wing partnership in the history of football. It might have started out as a magic moment, but before very long it became the very opposite. It was a muddy ground and I grew more and more tired as the match went on. It was one of these experiences which almost every professional I have ever met recognises, the first time you are thrown into the real world of league soccer and you find you are saying to yourself over and over again, 'I'll never be a footballer.' All you want to do is run away and hide. It seems impossible that you will ever be able to play the game as well as the men round about you.

I am sure every player feels like this on occasions, when no matter what you do, how hard you work, how much you run, the ball will just not go right for you. Your only hope is to play yourself out of this bad patch —although you should ask yourself if you are training hard enough or putting in the right amount of practice before you dismiss your off-games as mere bad luck. I was lucky that after my baptism in league soccer the Huddersfield manager, Mr Andy Beattie, kept me in the side and allowed me to find my feet.

One month after my first game for Scotland I was picked to play at Hampden—the greatest ground in the world for any Scottish footballer. That was a magic moment all right—in the stands were my mother and father watching me together for the very first time. In fact this was the first time I had ever appeared in front of a Scottish crowd, having gone straight from youth football in Aberdeen to Huddersfield. I noticed something as soon as I ran on to that huge field. The crowd was too large to be properly appreciated. Footballers notice small crowds because of the absence of atmosphere, but they don't seem to notice the huge crowd so much. Anyway, I felt very, very small as I took the field with the Scottish team—which was Brown (then Dundee), Grant (Hibernian), Caldow (Rangers); Mackay (then Hearts), captain, Toner (Kilmarnock), Docherty (then Arsenal); Leggatt (Fulham), Collins (then Everton), Herd (then Arsenal), Law and Henderson (then Arsenal).

Matt Busby was the Scottish manager and he told me

to mark Danny Blanchflower, the Irish right-half. We drew the game 2—2, although Scotland had been leading by two goals until very near the end. I was supposed to have carried out Mr Busby's instructions so relentlessly that Danny Blanchflower's legs were black and blue after the game. I must admit that I was younger and brasher in those days and went after every ball as though my life depended on it. This earned me some criticism, and although I don't play like that today I don't think it was a bad attitude for a young player to have.

I had few magic moments in Italy and if I was asked to recall the finest moment of my Italian career I would say it was the day I signed for Manchester United.

A game I remember as a great triumph for Scotland was the second leg of our World Cup-tie against Czechoslovakia at Hampden in 1961. The thrill of winning this match was later dimmed by the fact that we were defeated in the replay and knocked out of the World Cup, but that Hampden game stands on its own nevertheless. I was playing in Italy at the time and was recalled for this game to the Scottish team. The Czechs were four goals up from the first game. Scotland were twice behind and seven minutes from time we were drawing 2—2. (I had scored one of these.) Then I got the ball, hared past two Czech defenders, drew their goalkeeper, Schroif, and slipped the ball past him just at the post. Modesty does not prevent me from recalling that as we ran off the field the Czech team manager gave me a big hug and said, 'I salute the greatest player in the world.' He may have been indulging in psychological warfare, because in the deciding replay in Brussels we were beaten and Czechoslovakia went on to the final of the World Cup in Chile.

I must add that nothing ensures a bigger ribbing from my team-mates than seeing statements like 'the greatest player in the world' in the newspapers. There is no such thing. You cannot compare footballers like pop records in the hit parade.

There was a bit of the Top Twenty atmosphere about the big occasion at Wembley in 1964 when, to celebrate England's hundred years of soccer, the Rest of the World (F.I.F.A.) played England. To be considered one of the best players in the world was a great honour.

Soccer is a man's game and there are few occasions in which you are supposed to show emotion (which is why some people criticise the kissing that goes on after goals are scored—though they obviously don't appreciate the fantastic tension involved). Normally I don't like friendly games—this being a glamorous exception because nobody could fail to be thrilled at playing alongside Puskas and the rest. However, I've told you about this game already, and there is no point in going on and on about the past unless there is something positive to be learned.

To me tomorrow's game is always more important than the ones which are in the past. Soccer is a young man's game and it's probably just as well to leave memory lane to the veterans.

NINETEEN

FINALE

I hope that in some way or another this book can help you become a better footballer; even if it has made you think about certain parts of the game which had never occurred to you before it will have helped. Some men spend whole lifetimes in football as players and then managers and *they* will tell you that they never stop learning.

There is no one type of person who makes a better footballer than anyone else. Just an attitude. Players who work get on. Players who don't work don't get on. It has always been as natural for me to kick a ball as to breathe and I consider myself one of the luckiest people alive because I am able to earn my living doing the thing I enjoy most. This applies to every professional I know, for football is not a sport for half-hearted and the cynical.

Whether you become a professional footballer or not depends on many things. There are boys who live in the constant hope that they will be discovered by a talent scout. There are others, like myself, who are playing away in the school team without the slightest thought of ever doing anything more in soccer when suddenly they are whisked away into the tough, exciting world of the professional game.

The main thing is to play the game you enjoy and play it as well as you can—there is no real enjoyment in being bad at anything, in my opinion.

Football is a very simple game, basically. There are so-called 'experts' who clutter up our minds with fancy terms and high-sounding jargon, but to my mind they often speak 22-carat rubbish. The secret of playing football is to do the simple, obvious thing and to make sure you can do it faster than the other fellow.

Of course, some of you may have seen Manchester United playing and you may be saying to yourself, 'If Law knows so much about the game why doesn't he play like a genius every week?' If you do say that, I am glad, because it shows you at least grasp the gulf between theory and practice. Anybody can write a lot of technical advice on how to play football—but nobody can make *you* a footballer unless you are born to it.

At least one of my friends, Dave Mackay of Derby, says that the boy who is going to be a professional footballer has to start playing the game at the age of six or seven. It's too late at the age of twelve—in fact, round about that age most managers would be able to tell whether a boy has the basic talents necessary for the big game. I agree with Dave.

But there is an important point to make. Football is a great game—to my mind, the greatest in the world. It is great to play and great to watch (some of the time anyway). But any boy who gets the choice of playing or watching should have no hesitation in plumping for playing the game himself.

I know that I would be out of a job if every man and boy in Britain decided to kick a ball himself on Saturday afternoons and at first this might give me some headaches (I've never met a Scotsman yet who wanted to throw away money!), but it would not mean the end of my football. As long as I am able to walk I will always be looking for a chance to kick a ball about—even for the Old Crocks Eleven.

I hope the game gives you as much pleasure as it has given me. It can give you a lifetime's enjoyment, from the days of kicking a tennis ball in the street all the way down the years until you are a grand old stager who tells youngsters that they don't have players now like they had when you were young.

Football turned *me* from a skinny little kid with a squint into a man.

I sincerely hope it can do as much for you.